Couple Skills

25 Skills to Build a Deeper Connection with Your Partner, Improve Intimacy and Make your Relationship and Communication Work

Robin Wesley

Table of Contents

Introduction

Congratulations on choosing Couple Skills and thank you for doing so.

You are about to learn some of the most critical information needed to establish and maintain good communication in your relationship from the start. Breakdowns in and ineffective communication delivery can easily take your relationship down wrong paths that lead to an eventual split. You will learn ways to keep this from happening, even if you already feel like the relationship is on the brink of disaster. It can be saved!

How can a book make any difference in a relationship that seems filled with anger, disappointment, and conflict? You'll get strong, actionable advice that has worked for hundreds and thousands of people sharing the same struggles. You can begin working on problems TODAY!

Every chapter is FILLED with valuable ways that you AND your partner can work on the relationship in real time. Begin unlocking the potential that exists in your relationship. Rediscover the reasons you fell in love and find even deeper ways to connect. Learn how to safeguard your relationship from typical problems that tear most apart.

Discover a deeper way to show your partner how much you value their presence and input. You can begin the process of healing and come out of this a stronger, more resilient couple!

Chapter 1: Dialogue as the Foundation

Various methods of communication have always been observed in human interaction, whether it's by directly observing language in action, or through the compilation of stone etching or drawings done on the walls of caves, ancient buildings, or cliffsides. Dialogue is critical to making your ideas, feelings, and needs understood by those within your circle of influence. It's one of the most basic elements of establishing a good and strong relationship.

Daily Intimate Talking Time Matters

Most relationship counselors agree that every healthy couple needs to share at least 60 to 90-minutes of intimate time in conversation every day. It's important to check in with your partner and exchange information, provide emotional or mental support, and cultivate closeness. Don't let the busy moments of life rob you and your partner of this much-needed time to bond and set the tone for the relationship.

A few ways that you can find this critical time is to:

• Set the alarm early and get up to spend quality time in meaningful dialogue.

• Cook breakfast or dinner together and spend the time talking as you fix the food and eat.

• Turn off the television at night and opt for soft music, cuddling, and talking.

- Meet for brunch or lunch.

- Commute to work using one vehicle and talk on the way to and from the work sites.

Every day that you spend in deep, concentrated connection to your partner, the more you build on your feelings of partnership and communion. It's an actionable step in a relationship you must give time to in order to get the best results.

Continued Learning and Growing

All close relationships in life offer us the opportunity to expand our thinking and learn new things. The person we choose to partner with is no exception. You both bring qualities, knowledge, and skills to the relationship that are unique to you and can be shared with a curious and inquisitive partner. It's these differences that often attract us to another person. It's less about opposites attracting and more about finding someone that knows things or has abilities you do not. The want for completion is the driving desire. How often have you heard the exclamation, "You complete me!"

Nurturing the Bonds of Friendship

The most fulfilling relationships are often reported to be the ones that have taken the time to cultivate a strong bond of friendship. What does a friendship entail? It's generally a fair mix of emotional sharing, shared experiences, devoted time, and finding common ground, likes, or interests. It holds true whether you are talking about traditional friendships or in love relationships. The more you find to focus on that are positive, enjoyed activities and experiences for both partners, the easier it is to avoid conflict.

A strong bond of friendship can carry your relationship over some rough waters. You are less likely to jump to bad conclusions about a friend, refuse to compromise in situations, or do things to intentionally hurt them. It can easily translate into the same benefits for your relationship. Couples that nurture and invest time into strong friendship bonds will experience far fewer problems and resolve conflicts easier. You begin this process through dialogue about likes, dislikes, and finding what is shared.

Maintaining the Feelings of Team Effort

Good communication is the primary way you maintain the feeling of being on the same team. Life can get rough out there and you can each feel a bit battered for a variety of reasons. The relationship should always be the "port in the storm" type scenario, both mentally and literally. Cultivating importance in the support of your partner will produce longevity in your relationship.

What is the opposite of being on the same team? Is it being on opposing teams? Does it simply imply an indifference? To the one feeling slight betrayals or confusion over which team you're on, indifference can seem as bad as you're being the declared enemy. Verbally checking in with your partner daily is the most important ingredient to staying on the same team.

Expressing Emotion, Concern, or Conveyance of Information

Much like the use of dialogue in all facets of life, it allows each individual the ability to express emotions and feelings, offer our concerns and preferences, and convey all types of important information. Unless you are working the equivalent of two full-time jobs, you will be spending more time with your partner than anyone considered a co-worker. It makes good communication skills a necessity for peaceful co-existing.

Basic dialogue is how you let your partner know things like:

- The state of your health.
- Upcoming budget concerns.
- Bill due dates.
- Upcoming events and appointments.
- Work schedules.
- Questions about people, places, or things.
- Demonstrate whether you're happy, sad, mad, excited, etc.

At no point in a relationship does the need for dialogue and communication become unimportant. It should remain a vital skill that is continually worked on and evolved over the years. As you get to know your partner more, the easier you can adjust your communication methods to mesh in ways that require little effort.

How Lack of Dialogue Contributes to Feelings of Being Alone or Emotionally Abandoned

The following graph shows the number of people that have reported lack of communication being the primary reason for seeking professional couple's therapy and beginning thoughts of separation or divorce. It may not be the leading cause of divorce, but it does point to being the main reason to begin considering divorce. (See figure 1)

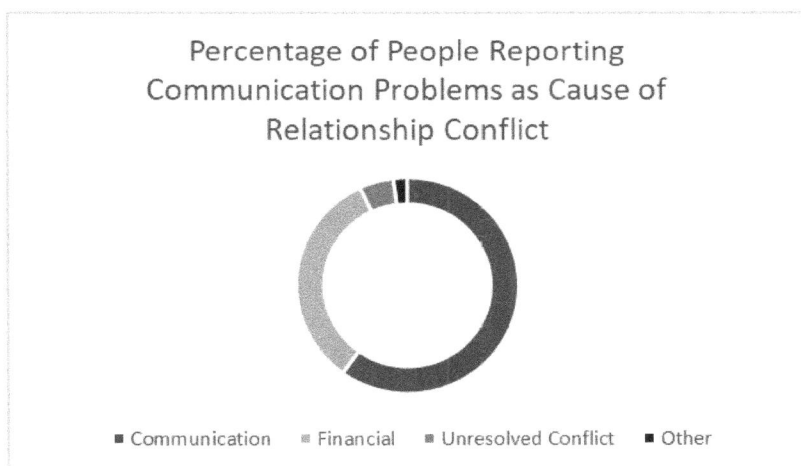

Percentage of People Reporting Communication Problems as Cause of Relationship Conflict

■ Communication   ▪ Financial   ■ Unresolved Conflict   ■ Other

Figure 1- Compiled statistics of reporting private couple's therapeutic professionals in 2017.

Financial reasons can also lead a couple to the brink of divorce but many times it's lack of communication that leads to an unexpected financial crisis. The importance of having and maintaining a good daily dialogue cannot be overstated in relationships. It's the best step you can take towards building a stronger and more lasting foundation.

Chapter 2: Open and Sincere Communication

Consistently using open and honest communication that comes from sincerity will get you further in life with all your endeavors and dealings with people. Getting in bad habits of placating people or only telling them what you feel will get you by or gives them the answers they crave is non-helpful. It can paint you into some interesting and uncomfortable corners. Instead of using flowery words, use words that count. Be specific in your language and clear in your delivery. Flattery is nice, but your partner usually wants to know exactly how you feel in all situations.

Why Clarity Matters

Not being clear about your communication and giving of information causes confusion. Confusion, in turn, leads to frustration. It can cause your partner to be late for important appointments, miss critical deadlines, or even worse, lose faith in what you tell them. The two biggest problems that arise from a lack of clear communication are misunderstandings and misinterpretations. Both can become huge stumbling blocks to the relationship when it becomes the norm.

Misunderstandings –

Having an important date or time wrong, giving your partner the wrong name of someone, an incorrect billing date, or other wrong information can lead to huge misunderstandings and sour consequences. A shutoff of power service, a missed doctor appointment, or feeling foolish at not knowing the correct name of someone you are calling back can all cause confusion, resentment, and momentary anger. TAKE NOTES and LEAVE NOTES that are detailed and provide more information than necessary to be safe.

Misinterpretations –

Facts are an important part of imparting the correct information through your communications. Anything less than a complete picture can cause your partner to try and fill in the blanks for themselves. It can lead to all sorts of bad experiences. Don't leave your partner guessing about anything. Be clear and direct in all your communications.

Complete Communications

Most verbal communication leads to an individual painting a picture in their mind of what has happened, needs to be done or some expected outcome. Having less than complete information can lead to the creation of visuals that are completely wrong. What good would it do to arrange to meet your partner for lunch but not tell them where? How fair is it to tell your partner that the budget is tight for the week, yet not say how much money is available for food shopping? It creates an impossible situation in which to succeed. You'll not be able to find the right place for lunch and you'll overspend the budget on food.

To continue with the budget example, you might wonder

why the budget is limited without having full details on where the money is being spent. You may not realize that it's time to pay a car payment or the mortgage. Full understanding of any situation comes from having the most complete information available.

Get Everything Out in the Open – Hide Nothing!

When you are in a relationship, certain expectations exist that you disclose everything. Anything that is viewed as "hiding" information can set off a virtual WW3. If the husband or wife is having to take a business trip and a member of the opposite sex will be going as well, say something. To not disclose this can be later construed as hiding the information for possibly nefarious purposes. You may not want to cause waves, but you can create a tsunami by not saying something from the start.

No matter how slight something seems, it's better to let your partner know the information. It can be a big mistake to try and filter out what you think is important or what you feel they can handle. You should always treat your partner as an adult and with respect. Hiding things, even for noble purposes, can backfire and make you appear dishonest.

You should also avoid hiding your feelings, concerns, worries, fears, and doubts. Rather than making you appear weak, it brings a more human quality to your personality. Part of the reason humans reach out to others and form relationships is to have that shoulder to lean on and constant partner in the battle of life. Hiding your emotions and other intimate thoughts are robbing you and your partner of full engagement.

When a Partner Feels Slighted or Ignored

How much time do you spend on quality communication? If your partner feels like they are always getting the tail-end of your day and never realize any good moments of deep conversation, they can begin to feel slighted or cheated. It might even get to the point that they build resentment or feel ignored. Even though days can be hectic and time short, make a special time to connect with your partner each day. Ensure its undisturbed and doesn't feel rushed. You might find your stress and worries of the day disappearing by doing this little routine.

Life has a way of getting so fast-paced it's easy to forget why you partnered up with someone. You can begin letting life fall out of balance and lose touch with what's important. Everyone needs a little time to themselves to decompress daily, but don't forget your partner in the fray. Find ways to reconnect each day to continue building the relationship. It's over years that the deepest connections are made, but it's done one day at a time.

Approaching Everything with Sincerity and Honesty

Honesty with your partner can never be achieved without being completely honest with yourself. You have to know how you feel about every circumstance encountered before you have the ability to honestly share those feelings, concerns, and ideas with a partner. The more honest you can be with your feelings and ideas, the better your partner can understand where you're coming from when making decisions or adding input.

Every communication effort you make with your partner that is done with honesty and sincerity should be received well. It sometimes depends on the situation and information being imparted, but generally, people prefer honesty over the alternative. When the information is tough and news bad, stick with integrity and give honest assessments and information. A million ways exist to use the right words to soften a blow, but nothing can replace honesty.

Chapter 3: The 2 Basic Fundamental Aspects of Harmonious, Symbiotic Relationships

Two basic fundamentals exist when it comes to communication and having a harmonious relationship with your mate. A symbiotic relationship is one in which both partners fit well and work seamlessly together for the common good. Learning how to master these fundamentals will almost guarantee you can reach beyond and become conversational experts. What you will score for sure is more peace in your daily lives. Each person will feel valued for who they are and what they think or feel.

Are You Listening? No, REALLY Listening?

Listening is one of the most important communication skills you can develop. Without it, conversations will fall flat. Everything will always be about you and your concerns. A relationship needs the involvement of the partner in every aspect of the other person's life out of interest and desire. Obligation should not be a part of the picture. If your partner feels you only listen because you have to, you'll find opportunities to grow the relationship to be limited. (See figure 2)

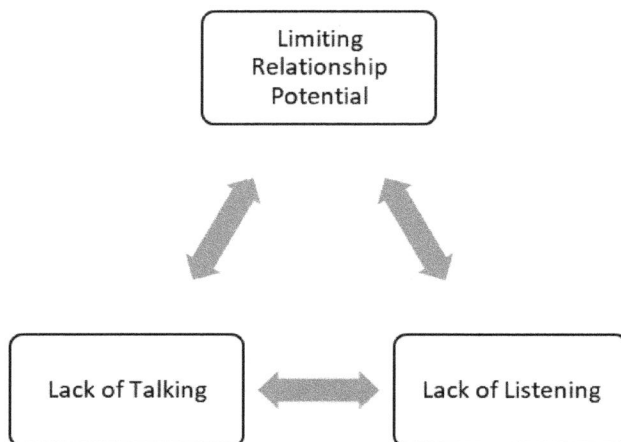

Figure 2 – The cycle that leads to consistent relationship limitations.

Body Language of Listening –

Body language can have a great deal to do with our own ability to listen to a partner. It signals to ourselves as much as the partner the depth at which you are willing to give full concentration to what's being said.

A few signs that you aren't interested in the conversation are:

- Lack of eye contact.
- Being prodded for a response.
- Turning away to continue with another activity.
- Partner having to repeat information.

It's possible that some conversations happen during busy times that are not optimal for the best conversational manners, but you should always to try and make this the exception, rather than the rule. Be aware of your body language and signaling and that it doesn't give unintended signals that you are too busy to talk to your partner.

Lose the Distractions –

Distractions come in all forms and fashion, but the worst are the smart devices that seem to have the population enslaved. Set your tablet or smartphone down when talking with your partner. Videos, texts, emails, and games can wait for a few minutes. You and your partner both deserve a little quality time to talk without interruptions and distractions. It might require going somewhere private or talking at odd hours. Whatever works to get you the time necessary without the usual distractions.

Does Your Partner KNOW You're Listening? -

Are you openly letting your partner know that you're listening? Try and face your partner and look at them when having a dialogue. It helps you focus on what's being said. You could also:

• Ask questions to let them know you are hearing what is being said.

- Repeat back important points.

- Be expressive with your facial muscles.

- Offer support or solutions.

Try exercising the skills you desire when talking to someone else. What are the things you notice that makes you recognize they are paying attention to what you're saying? Implement them at every opportunity when talking with your partner. You will make them feel that their words hold real value for you.

Are You Talking? No, REALLY Talking?

The difference in talking "at" someone and "with" someone is in the level of joint participation. Having someone talk "at" you come off as more of a lecture and can even cross the border into nagging, depending on the topic of conversation. Talking "with" someone is expecting a response, at least periodically. True conversations are ones that involve more than one person on equal footing. Most participants will switch roles between speaker and listener several times during the discussion. As simple as it might seem to say you are always talking, is it a true talking session or talk-at session?

Finding Quality Time –

Good conversations will require finding quality time to spend with your mate. It can be at a time you would normally watch television or switch off the set and go for a walk. Talk over a leisurely breakfast or as you get ready for bed. The more relaxed the setting, the more you'll enjoy your conversations. Try putting on some relaxing music or pour a glass of wine in the evening. Sit out on the patio and take in the fresh air. Build as much relaxation into time as possible.

Don't Rush Your Partner –

Another reason for choosing a good time for communicating is to avoid you or your partner from feeling rushed to get through an important conversation. Rushing is when critical details are left out or many things get left unsaid. Your partner might give up trying to discuss things with you if they feel consistently rushed through conversations. It's a way of giving them the hint that their words hold less value, whether it's your intention or not. Pick times that are not as stressed and stretched for time when possible. Give them all the time they need to feel comfortable enough to say whatever is on their mind.

Don't Discourage Conversation -

You might not be interested in the topic or it brings you feelings of dread but try not to discourage conversations and make topics off-limits to your partner. Every individual in a relationship needs to feel as if they have a voice. Discouraging open conversation can lead to feelings of depression and loneliness. It's something you want to guard against and encourage an openness that gives your mate a safe zone to discuss whatever is on their mind.

Chapter 4: Showing Your Partner Appreciation and Gratitude

It's both nice and necessary to show your partner appreciation and gratitude when they do things for you. Many people have gotten away from showing basic courtesy with things like saying a verbal "thank you." It should go beyond this when it comes to your life partner. The more gratitude you show, the more energy they will expend on the relationship. Both men and women respond equally well to a good dose of thankfulness and gratitude.

The Big Deal in Partner Appreciation

Why is feeling gratitude and showing appreciation to your partner important? It lets them know you recognize their sacrifice of time, money, or expertise it took to get something done, giving you a present, or in another way benefit you. It's a more assured way of knowing it will happen again if you show the right level of appreciation. Showing gratitude is a way of offering an affection for your partner that is deeper than most others.

The first few years of a relationship are filled with times that are often clouded by self-doubt. Are you doing right by your partner? Do they feel appreciated for everything they do? It's especially true of relationships that are important, and you want to last. Any individual that cares for their partner will be looking to improve communication of appreciativeness at every opportunity.

Saying and Demonstrating Thankfulness

Cooking you a hearty and healthy meal, doing the laundry, picking the kids up from school, picking up a few things from the grocery store, or taking out the trash are all things that can easily be taken for granted. Getting in the habit of seeking out your partner to personally thank them for doing something, saying something, or otherwise helping you. The thank you will go a long way towards making you a prime target to receive even more good things from your partner. It separates you from those that want what they want without any consequent.

Giving Your Partner Adequate and Appropriate Recognition

Did you come home to a clean bathroom yet haven't found the time to thank your partner for doing the dirty work? You can always stop what you're doing and hunt them down in your house or apartment and give them an immediate thank you. Having a partner that can kick it into gear and get things done as needed is a rare quality that you want to reward.

Dividing up chores seems like a fair thing to do, but what if you or your mate is called into work more often during the week? Taking on more household chores might be the thing to do to make it fair and balanced. Make sure you give your partner credit and thanks for pulling extra duty. It's another sign of team effort that should be given the proper recognition.

Communicating Appreciation Through Verbalizing to Partner and Others

How hard is it to stop and say "thank you" to someone? Constantly doing things for someone, even if it's your spouse or partner, can become off-putting if they can't seem to muster an occasional "thanks." It's two words put together that can make your day when coming from the right person. It recognizes that someone went out of their way to make something happen. It doesn't have to be anything grand, but make it seem as if you were given a million dollars.

You can and should go one step further. Let your friends and family know how awesome they are in what they did. You don't have to go overboard but imagine how nice it seems compared to most complaining that couples do about the other behind their backs. Provide a refreshing change. Make the one you love feel special in the moment. You are guaranteed to get a repeat performance the next time help is needed.

Easy Ways to Show Appreciation and Gratitude

Showing a little appreciation and gratitude can be as easy as saying "thank you" but here are a few other ways you can make them feel special:

- Fix their favorite meal.
- Purchase an afternoon massage.

- Plan a weekend away.

- Go for a surprise picnic.

- Set up a nice bubble-bath.

- Take them out to dinner.

- Get some flowers.

- Write a heartfelt note.

- Go to the movies.

You may not be able to things like this all of the time, but occasionally it can make a positive impact. It helps keep the relationship fresh and exciting. Your partner will begin to look forward to your creative and appreciative side.

Chapter 5: Make a Date – and KEEP IT!

Becoming a couple doesn't mean you have to skip the dating phase. You may have the person you've always searched for but now is not the time to give up on romance and gaining private time. You need to continue doing activities you've always enjoyed, even if you are working on your 50th year together. One of the secrets to long and healthy marriages is to always spend quality alone-time with the one you love. It shouldn't involve family, friends, kids, or anything else.

Why You Need to Set Aside Time for Your Partner

Most people don't have a problem taking training courses, attending college, and reading up on things to improve their knowledge for a career. Many people hardly raise an eyebrow at making an appointment for a teeth cleaning or oil change on the car. Why is it that very little time is devoted to setting date plans with your partner? A relationship is an investment that requires a little input now and again to keep the dividends rolling through the door.

Your time might seem exceptionally limited if you work full time or are running your own business. Every minute counts in these moments. The problem with not placing adequate emphasis on spending time with your partner is that you can begin to drift apart. A sudden loss in companionship can begin to take away that warm and fuzzy feeling you had at the start. Your partner might begin to feel they are in the way and unimportant. Rather than telling them it couldn't be further from the truth, it's better to show them by making plans and sticking with them no matter what.

Fitting Dates into a Busy Schedule

The easiest way to fit dates into the busiest schedules is to do things in the course of what you would be doing anyway. If you normally eat breakfast before heading to work, get up earlier and go out to eat. Meet up for lunch at a location convenient for both. Sneak off for an early dinner and a movie if it's a grocery shopping day. The produce will still be there when you're done.

It sometimes requires quite a bit of pre-planning and travel in different vehicles to make it all work. It's worth the time spent trying to figure it all out. The adventure seems sweeter and has more meaning when the time if hard-fought to find and get for special occasions and dates.

Partner Only Events

It seems like there is always someone trying to "crash in" on your planned outing. Friends or family might try and invite themselves along. You and your partner need to be firm in keeping this time reserved for only the two of you. An extra co-worker along for lunch might seem harmless, but it takes away from the special nature of the time and defeats your main purpose.

The same goes for any children involved. Find a babysitter or have friends and family care for children when you go out to the movies, dinner, theater or another event. Family time can be arranged for a later date. It's just as important to have quality couple's time to maintain a strong and healthy relationship.

Drop Your Partner Off Some Food if Stuck at the Office

No matter how well you plan some days, at times the job has to come first. If your plans are foiled by the sudden need of your partner to eat in at the office, go out and get some healthy food for them to eat and drop it off. It lets them know you understand and still want to see their needs are met. Hopefully, it's not the result of every date plan. The occasional work emergency can't be helped.

If you are unable to drive the distance alone and make it back in time for your job, see if there is a local eatery that will deliver some great food and pay by phone with a debit or credit card. The extra effort will not go unnoticed by your partner.

Only Allow Extreme Emergencies to Cancel Plans

What are allowable reasons to cancel plans? Having a rough day at work or feeling tired is not always a good excuse. The relaxation time you'll get when keeping the plans will make all of that disappear. You'll be glad to stick it through. A few acceptable reasons for cancellation are:

- Illness or medical emergency.

- Unable to get child care.

- Unexpected visitors.

- The event is canceled.

- Vehicle breakdowns.

- Bad/dangerous weather.

- Other unspecified family emergencies.

You might still be able to work around some events like a vehicle breakdown or unexpected visitors. If you get the car to a shop and take another or the visitors leave early enough, the rest of the night is yours! Staying flexible and being creative is the key to enjoying more dating success.

Reschedule Right Away

If things come in the way of your plans, don't wait for weeks to find another opportunity. Reschedule your date right away. Find another event or pick another movie and try it again and soon as possible. Truly reserve cancellation for only the most important things. You need to demonstrate to your partner that you value spending time with them. Leave no doubts that you could have found a way around a situation.

Pick less stressful events or venues if you feel extremely tired or stressed. Grab a nice take-out meal and head to a beautiful park if the weather is nice. You can incorporate the relaxation that nature provides along with spending time with the one you love.

Chapter 6: Create Shared Rituals

E veryone brings a semblance of ritual and tradition into a relationship. The problem is, there's never any room for two and rarely are two people raised from the same situation and circumstance. You might have been married before and have certain ritual ways you celebrate anniversaries or holidays. Your partner might have grown up as an only child and is not used to sharing space. Coming from different worlds can cause friction, or it can be viewed as a great starting point for a new life.

The Blending of Two World's

A serious relationship that leads to marriage will mean blending all of your individual family rituals, traditions, beliefs, and values. It's often easier to let many of them go and simply start from scratch. The reasons you carefully consider the values and beliefs of the other person when embarking on a relationship path becomes painfully clear at this point. When base-line values, goals, and beliefs are too off, the relationship will struggle. It's commonly referred to as being unevenly yoked and can spell disaster for the future plans of the relationship.

It doesn't mean that the mountains are impassable. All you have to do is look for the right valleys and paths to make your way over, around, and through them. Every serious relationship has had to deal with these issues, but many didn't give it much thought beforehand. It's hard to see the possible warning signs of future conflict when everything seems to be fun, new, and exciting. Eventually, the reality of the situation sets in and you learn that forming your own rituals and traditions is usually the easier path.

The Importance of Rituals and Traditions

Rituals and traditions rule your life more than you might think of at the moment. It amounts to almost every repeated action we take, whether it's holiday times, special days, or an everyday meal. Let explore what some of these are, so you can have a better picture of what you will have to deal with when blending lives.

What are Rituals? –

Rituals are actions you take regularly, usually on a daily or weekly basis. Some of these are lifelong and hard to break. A few examples of rituals are:

• Sitting down at the table for meals or eating in front of the television.

• Daily exercise routine.

• Jogging or walking each day.

• Certain days for chores like laundry or vacuuming.

What are Traditions? –

Traditions are things you do, places you go, and specialty items you eat or drink for special occasions. Holidays are normally filled with traditions.

A few examples are:

- New Year's Eve and Champagne.
- Birthday dinner out.
- Thanksgiving meal prep at home or with family.
- Valentine's Day expectations.
- Christmas gift opening.

All individual rituals and traditions will have to be explored to see if you have some common ground. Many times, the traditions and rituals must be replaced for ones that work best for both of you.

Holidays, Birthdays and Anniversaries

Unless you are a couple that doesn't care to celebrate any holidays, anniversaries, or birthdays, you will have to do some work to try and blend the traditions that are favorable to the both of you. Each will come with their own experiences and family traditions and the results will be something new that is either a hybrid of both or a completely new creation. (See figure 3)

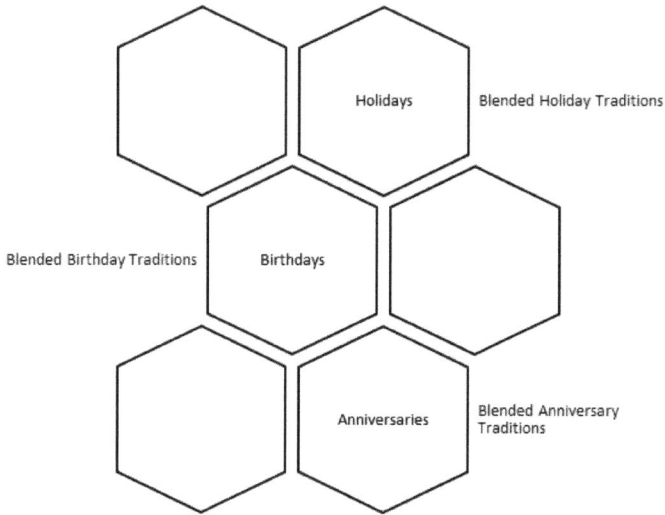

Figure 3 – Blending traditions.

One example of blending traditions is when you enjoy cooking a nice birthday meal, but your partner cannot cook. You can always blend the traditions. You cook their birthday meal and they take you out to a restaurant for yours. It's the perfect blend and solution.

Creating Memories and Standards

The important part of coming together as a couple is to communicate about what is enjoyable to you about certain rituals and traditions. No matter how you decide to proceed as a couple, make great memories and set the standards you want for your own new family. You can completely veer from all the rituals and traditions you know and establish new ones.

Create More than You Borrow

A fun and enjoyable part of becoming a solid couple is to establish new traditions and rituals that are distinctly your own. Borrowing the parts that are an important part of your past and incorporating them can be done, but make sure you discuss everything to the point of being comfortable with any decisions. Create new rituals and traditions based on the things you love to do and are important as a couple. Where will your new combined interests take you? Maybe you will begin taking summer vacations and make that a tradition. Perhaps it will be sitting at a favorite café on the weekends drinking a latte. It's all up to you and your partner.

Appreciate the New Traditions and Rituals

Enjoy and appreciate all of the new traditions and rituals, as well as any blended ones you design for your joint lives. Your life together will continue to evolve, and the daily communication practiced will help you change things up as you see fit. You might have to continue with some rituals and traditions on your own. It's fine as long as you develop a healthy number of ones you can enjoy together.

Chapter 7: Be Playful Together

The occasional pillow fight, the game of tag in the yard, and the piggy-back ride can help keep your relationship fresh, youthful, and fun. Establishing some level of playful interaction every day is important to defeating the boredom that can settle over a lifetime of seeing each other daily. The more effort you place in this endeavor, the better the rewards are for a lifetime.

Playful Morning and Evening Banter

Let's face it when both partners have to work several days a week, the most likely times to spend a few moments around each other is in the morning and evening. Add a bit of playful conversational banter to your normal routines of making breakfast, drinking coffee, or settling in for an evening in front of the television.

It's the perfect time to tell your partner about the funny things that happened during your day, a crazy dream from the night before, or find a couple of funny videos to stream on your smartphone. You can look up lists of bizarre and funny trivia. Anything to leave you and your partner laughing is the right direction to go.

Choose Enjoyable Activities

Both partners should partake in choosing and planning enjoyable activities, but don't wait around for the other person to make the first move. Talk with them about the intended goal of livening things up and begin planning strategic activities that are fun for both of you. It's time to stretch your limits and get involved in new things. You can try:

• Adopting a dog and taking it for daily walks to a local park.

• Complete a paint-by-number set together.

• Find a cafe that serves root beer floats and gets one to share.

• Take horse riding lessons together.

• Work out together at a local fitness center.

Most of the activities you find can be relatively close to home and cost little in the way of money. The investment of time is priceless. You will both walk away feeling more fulfilled in the relationship.

Enjoying Consensual Touch

The occasional pat on the rump, quick hug, shoulder rub, or kiss on the back of the neck is a great way to add instant connections when your partner is receptive to consensual touching. Human touch has healing properties that go beyond the current understanding of medical science. You can literally help one another stay healthier and build a robust immune system by incorporating frequent touch into your everyday lives.

Give your partner an unexpected foot massage after a hard day on their feet. Cuddle on the couch in the evening while watching a good movie. Offer one another a full-body massage at bedtime. It will help induce a good rest and might lead to fun places before the lights go out.

Unexpected Road Trips

Keeping an element of surprise is another way to liven up and keep the relationship fresh. Your partner will never know what to expect. Plan ahead for an unexpected road trip to go sightseeing, take in an event, or just get away from it all. You can have a specific destination in mind or wing it and drive. The whole point is to take in what you can for the day and end up back home for the evening. You can try things like:

- Drive a scenic highway.
- Tour a historic town, museum, or art gallery.
- Check out a local festival or concert.
- Pick your own fruit from a local orchard.
- Go fishing.
- Hiking.
- Kayaking.
- Canoeing.
- Go on a boat day cruise.

It's important to find a babysitter for the kids and go without family or friends. It's a time to take the day and spend every moment together doing fun things or taking in beautiful sights.

It will take a little more planning to get away for an entire weekend but it's worth the effort. Soaking in some time of ultimate relaxation can be refreshing for your relationship and help take away the stress of daily living. It's like squeezing in a mini-vacation to a busy schedule. You will be somewhat limited on places you can go since you don't want your drive time to exceed 4-hours. Anything more will crunch your time and make it all seem like more work than it's worth. Depending on location, you can try:

- Spend the weekend at a beach-side resort.
- Rent a small cabin in the woods.
- Pitch a tent and spend the weekend camping.
- Stay the weekend at a luxury resort and spa.

Spend every possible moment reconnecting and rekindling the sparks of your relationship. Check the weather reports if you plan to stay outdoors and make alternative plans if it's not suitable for camping or being at the beach.

Pick a Day to Pamper Your Partner

Another way to incorporate some fun in your relationship is to plan ahead for a day your partner will be home and surprise them with a full day of pampering. Begin by sneaking out of bed early, make a tasty breakfast and serve it in bed. Set the rules so that nothing even close to work is to be done and they are the King or Queen for the entire day. Wives – take your husband out to get a haircut and shave. Husbands – take your wife to get her hair and nails done. The joy it brings to your partner will make it all worthwhile.

Chapter 8: Know When to Say "No" and When to Accept "No"

Have you lost sight as to when it's okay to say or accept the word "no?" Conflict can and will arise if there are no established boundaries. The way we learn the boundaries is to test them and define them so that your partner is never in the dark. Issues can arise when partners fail to agree on joint decisions or one feels they always have to capitulate. Learning and creating the right boundaries will keep everyone happy. Seeing things from the eyes of your partner can help make joint decisions easier.

Saying "No" and Creating Healthy Boundaries

Women in relationships are at the highest risk of over-promising time and trying to take on too much for fear of saying "no" when it would be perfectly reasonable to do so. One example is when both partners are working a full-time job and have children. A woman will often take on the nurturer role and prepare the meal, make sure homework is done, dishes washed, and kids bathed. If the husband asks nicely for her to press his shirt for work the next day, should she say "yes?" It's certainly fine if she feels up to it, but with a staggering amount of work done after clocking out, it's perfectly fine to say "no."

It works the same in reverse. If your husband has worked a long day, is it fair to demand he mow the lawn, paint the back room, and reorganize the garage in one afternoon? If he has the stamina and energy, fine. It's also okay to say "no" when it stacks up and it's an unreasonable amount of work at one time. Maintaining a healthy balance and boundaries is important.

When is it Good to Say "No?"

The reasons to say "no" can be as numerous as the ones to say "yes." You might always want to be seen as the one that gets along with everyone and will do whatever it takes to not "make waves," but is it worth taking on too much? It can and will eventually lead down the road to resentment and arguments. Anytime something is going against your personal boundaries, such as not wanting help with every little problem you mention or feeling put upon with your limited time, it is right to step back and say "no."

You can find a way to say "no" that is non-confrontational and allows you to set and maintain healthy limits and boundaries. The purpose of establishing a lifelong relationship is not to put so much burden on yourself that you can't function. It will end up breaking you down in the long-run. It's better to learn to say "no" at the appropriate times from the start.

When You or Your Partner See the Bigger Picture

Coming to the table to make joint decisions can be tough in some situations. You and your partner could be at odds over the purchase of a new car, making a big relocation move, or starting a family. It's usually the larger, earth-shattering decisions that prove the most difficult. Take a step back and calmly try and see the situation from the eyes of your partner. Are they seeing something that you aren't?

Is it possible you are swept up in the excitement of thinking about a new car, new baby, or a brand-new home in a new location? What will a major move entail? Is a large purchase going to put a major hit on the budget? How will starting a family affect the household income? Is it even possible at the moment? Make sure that the decisions being made are sensible and reflect the team effort involved in running a household. Your partner might be looking at things in a more sensible light.

When You Should Gracefully Accept "No"

Couples that are comprised of partners that were "only children" and somewhat spoiled will have a hard time hearing "no" on occasion. It's possible to be so wrapped up in personal wants and desires that it's easy to forget the other person has feelings, wants, and their own desires in life. Maybe your husband can't stand the thought of a pink kitchen. Maybe your wife is tired of tripping over the toolbox in the den. Bringing in one more tool might be the start of a huge argument that could have been avoided by accepting the word "no."

If your partner seems to have valid reasons to say "no" it might be wise to roll with that answer. It's never smart to try and be the winner in every situation and the controller of the outcome for every decision. Coming to a happy medium is the best way to approach the more volatile decisions that have to be made. Understand that your partner might be worried about the finances with big purchases. It could be an instance where they love their job and aren't prepared to move away or find themselves unwilling to start a family at the moment. Big and important decisions have to be made together.

Avoiding the "People-Pleaser" Mentality

"People-pleasing" as a way of life ensures your partner will never have to worry about your saying "no," but your relationship satisfaction and happiness might be dubious at times. Learn to recognize when this a quality you or your partner possess. What does the "people-pleaser" mentality look like? A few examples are:

"Where would you like to eat?"

"Oh, it doesn't matter. I'm not picky."

"Which movie do you want to see?"

"You pick one. I'm fine with whatever."

"What would you like to go do?"

"You pick. It doesn't matter to me."

It could be that you really aren't that picky and choosy about things. Your partner might be expressing their desire to have your help in making the decision. Rarely do people not have specific foods and tastes in activities and movies. Your unwillingness to express this can become a source of frustration to your partner. They are looking for boundaries that you seem unwilling to set.

Maintaining Individuality Within the Pairing

Part of the reason you need to be able to say and accept "no" is to help maintain the individuality of both you and your partner within the pairing. It should become easy over time to work within the boundaries set to enjoy some individual preferences and be flexible enough to allow them the same. No one wants to be in a relationship with a robotic person. You had a distinct personality when you met, and they expect it to remain intact, even as you become a couple.

Chapter 9: The Art of Negotiation and Compromise

No two people can live in the same household day-in, day-out, over a period of years, without learning how to both compromise and negotiate. Negotiation is not always possible, but compromise should never be one-sided. The goals should never be that of deprivation or sacrifice, but one of providing for the needs and wants of both in a variety of ways that are fair and balanced. An alpha partner should never strive to always "get their way." Neither should the more beta partner give in an excessive amount. Both hardline positions have their own problems.

What's the Difference in Negotiation and Compromise?

Compromise is a process of agreeing to give something up in order to reach a common point of agreement between two parties or individuals. A good compromise is one that is done in a positive light and for the benefit of the entire situation. It's the right way to handle some situations in which you and your partner find yourself at odds, but not too far apart. One example is if you both want to go out to dinner but can't seem to agree on the time. You want to go earlier in order to get home and watch a movie that's on at a specific time. Your partner wants to go later because they hate driving through heavy traffic. You can come to a compromise by leaving slightly later to avoid the worst of traffic and set the DVR to make sure the movie is recorded in case you are late getting back home.

Negotiation is a bit different. It's used to incorporate a little compromise and leveraging to get exactly what you want and a little more when the gap is much larger between acceptable terms. One example of this is if when planning to go and meet with friends, your partner says they can't stand being around "X" and "Y", but "Z" is okay. You tell them "X" is coming along, but you can invite two of your friends to help distract you from your dislike of "Y." In this negotiation, you are both able to hang out with your preferred friends at the same time and everyone is a winner.

Why Both are Needed Skills in a Successful Relationship

You will have times that come around where strong compromise and negotiation skills are required in order to keep the peace. Not everyone will be on the same page at all times. Whether it's due to a lack of common interest, personality clashes with friends, difficult relationships with vital family members, situations will arise that necessitate negotiation. It's not bad skills to learn for life anyway. It can be used in almost any circumstance, including dealing with other friends, family, co-workers, and more.

Compromise Should Involve Both Sides Giving to Meet in the Middle

Compromise in a relationship should always be fair and balanced. Both sides should be willing and able to give something in order to achieve a final objective. The compromise should also be done in a positive way. You should always strive to not let anyone person sacrifice what they feel is important to achieve this peace. It's done in a fair, equitable, and balanced way. (See figure 4)

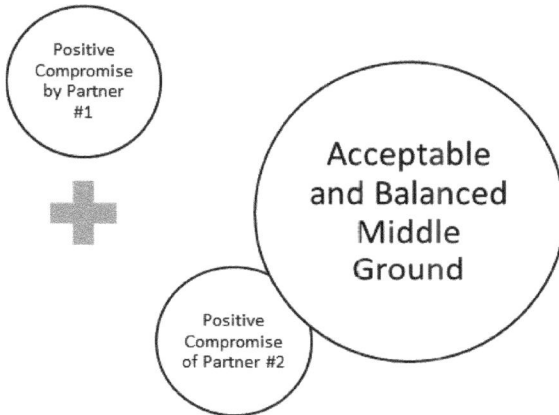

Figure 4 – The elements of a fair and balanced compromise.

In the above example of a compromise in leaving to go to dinner, a time was found that allowed the partner concerned with heavy traffic to go at a less busy time and the partner concerned with missing the movie could rest at ease with it being recorded if they failed to return by the time it started. Neither one sacrificed anything to achieve a balanced solution.

Negotiation is a Higher-Level Way to Get What You Both Want

The art of negotiation takes more time and planning to get the desired result, but anyone can learn to master it well with their partner. You will begin to think in terms of possible negotiation scenarios as you get more comfortable with their likes and dislikes versus your own. It's impossible to live a life of relationship bliss without knowing how to both compromise and negotiate for resolutions.

Never Discuss Compromise or Negotiation When Angry

Things never go well when try and reach a compromise or negotiate when one or both partners are angry. It's hard for everyone to get past emotions and focus on a real solution. Take some time and let anger pass before attempting to negotiate any type of compromise. It's difficult when it involves tough subjects like dealing with ex-spouses or family gatherings when the family dislikes your partner. Solutions are possible, but all details have to be considered.

Involve a Mediator if You Get Stuck

If the situation seems hopeless and you cannot seem to get past the problem and find a solution, locate a good mediator to assist. You can use the help of a mediation service or ask an impartial friend or relative to help you sort things out. It's vital to ensure you use someone that won't slant things in either individual's favor. It also should be someone that isn't prone to gossip. Try and keep any disagreements you have between the two of you.

Chapter 10: Keep the Parents Out of the Picture

W hen it comes to parents, it's hard to find a total balance in how they react to every situation. More often than not, the parents will take the side of their son or daughter over that of their partner. It's true with most family members. It's good to have an ongoing healthy relationship with parents, but it's essential that they not be involved in any decision-making for your household. If your partner feels they are heavily influencing decisions, you could be in for some rough waters.

Don't Force Your Partner to Attend Every Family Event

When relationships are rocky between you and your partner's parents, or between your partner and your own parents, don't force the issue on attending every family event. You can hit the big ones like birthdays, holidays, and anniversaries, but feel free to skip out on recurring Sunday night dinner. Remember, this is a time to begin making your own traditions and rituals. If everyone gets along fine, then feel free to spend more time together. Check with your partner before committing to anything. You might find resentment building if they feel forced because you already promised their attendance.

Don't Let Parents Guilt You into Things

Making you feel guilty about not being able to see you as much as before or not wanting to spend time with anyone, but you are setting a terrible precedent that you need to nip in the bud quickly. You can end up feeling like someone is dragging you by your heartstrings if it goes on for a long period of time. It's a type of conditioning that can have you running in circles and your partner furious. It leads to hiding phone calls, sneaking in lunches, and all sorts of situations that will end up making you feel guilty and that you're doing something wrong. Let your parents understand you are now a packaged deal. It makes them come to the conclusion that they have to give your partner a chance.

Parents CAN Behave Badly

Don't immediately discount what your partner says if they are reporting an incident of mistreatment by a parent. Parents CAN behave badly, especially if they feel they can bully your partner away. It's more common with parents who have a controlling nature and it can lead to some real arguments for you at home. You will tend to try and defend the parents, which might be in the complete wrong. Always validate the feelings of your partner. Empathize with the experience they've had and offer to talk with the offending party. Your partner will feel better by your listening and validating how awful they feel about the situation.

Get them to Back Off

One thing to watch out for are heated exchanges that can turn ugly in no time. If you find your partner under heavy attack for little or no reason, it's only right to step in and have them back off. Get the two parties separated, whether it means leaving a family function or having the parents leave your home. It's best to separate everyone until the situation calms down. You don't want to end up with anyone getting hurt or in jail over flared tempers.

Don't Tell Parents Every Juicy Detail of Your Lives

You can end up bringing in problems with parents by giving too many details about the goings on within your household. It's best to keep some things to yourself. Parents will feel naturally drawn towards protecting and defending their grown child. It's the way humanity works. Some parents are able to look at things objectively, especially over time. Don't expect that for the first few months or even years.

Don't Change Plans for Parents

Another expected event with parents that try to be more controlling than necessary is to show up at unexpected times. You should never set the precedent to cancel travel or other plans to accommodate this situation. Family emergencies and illness are another story, but to simply pop up out of nowhere unexpectedly is unfair to your relationship. Make sure you set the boundaries and ground rules firm from the start.

Don't Run to Parents for Advice - Ask Your Partner

Adding stress to your relationship is also a guarantee by consistently running to your parents for advice you should be seeking from your partner. It leaves your partner feeling as if you either don't trust or value their input. It tends to fade over time to some extent, especially if your parents come around to accepting your mate, but it can be the cause for some explosive arguments if they are barely on speaking terms. Always make it a priority to ask your partner for advice FIRST and never make plans to take action on anything without consulting with your partner.

Be Wary of Drama and Overdramatization of Events

Both partners are the better judge of their own parent's behaviors. Be careful with including parents in information about situations that can become over-amplified and dramatized. If your parents are renowned for making mountains out of molehills, don't let them know about the latest disagreement with your partner. Try not to diffuse situations that are creating drama or being used to stir up a bunch of turmoil and chaos. Keep your home an area of peace, not a constant war zone.

Chapter 11: Placing Friends in the Background

The best-case scenario is when all of your friends and the friends of your partner love you as much as they love your mate. It will happen occasionally but rarely is it true for every friend and every situation. Friends might begin to wonder why your time is being taken up so much with your partner, especially if they are not in a relationship. It can quickly become a point of contention that brings unneeded stress to your life.

Friends and Friction

Relationships evolve out of the desire for partners to spend increasing amounts of time around one another, often forgoing the presence of anyone else. It can seem like a shock to friends that are used to spending all of the time they want at your residence or out doing favorite activities. You suddenly have less time available, which can strike up feelings of insecurity, loneliness, or abandonment by close friends. It's important to allow them to feel included at times, but you also need to give the healthiest part of your time to your partner. If the feelings of resentment and insecurity aren't too drastic, it's a situation that can work when you make the right moves.

Leaving Childhood Friends Behind – Is It Necessary?

As much as you and your partner want all friendships to remain intact, it may reveal itself to be an impossible situation. You have to draw a figurative line in the sand for behaviors that are intolerable. You need to stay in close communication with your partner in regard to how you and they are being treated by friends. You might want to consider a calm confrontation or begin cutting ties if:

- Friends begin to make crude remarks or sexual advances towards your partner.
- Friends are hostile towards you or your partner.
- They bring constant negativity.
- They make increasing demands on your time.
- They tell lies to your partner to try and make them angry towards you.

You might be able to salvage the situation if you have an open and honest discussion with friends about bad behaviors, but there are times that friendships have to go if you want to stay with your chosen partner.

Eliminating the Third-Wheel Syndrome

Try being more low-key about any plans you have if you find friends suddenly showing up at the same restaurants or events and inviting themselves to hang out. Nothing seems more miserable on a date night than having an unexpected and unwanted third-wheel. You can offer to do a double-date if they want to plan ahead of time and it's comfortable for your partner. You will eventually have to begin being somewhat secretive of special plans with individuals that won't take a subtle hint. Make sure that schedule some time to spend with them on down the line. You don't want your friends to feel you have completely forgotten about them.

Why can't everyone just get along?

Personality clashes can also be a huge problem that makes it nearly impossible to be around their friends or have your partner around your friends. It's rarely a group of individuals. You might have one that lets you know constantly how much they can't stand your mate. Unless the friend begins to modify their language and behavior, the friendships tend to fade off. If they truly can't stand you or your partner, they will begin to wean themselves away from your presence. It generally is a problem that takes care of itself.

Making Peace with BFFs

Best friends forever. How often have you heard that term? It's worth taking the time to try and work the situation out if it's a friend that you or your partner has great affection for and have maintained a lengthy friendship. Good friends are hard to come by in a disposable world. Do your best to make your partner's friends feel welcome and included in appropriate events. Avoid rolling your eyes, sighing, or making negative comments when they are around. Remember them on holidays and for their birthday.

Little steps like this can begin to endear you to them and you'll find their doubts fade away. It eases all manners of insecurity if you keep an open dialogue and demonstrate your care for your partner.

Don't Drag Friends in on Relationship Troubles

Do your level best to not drag friends in on relationship problems. What could be a simple misunderstanding or temporary problem can be blown out of proportion by overly-concerned friends. It forces them to stick with loyalties and makes it unfair to your partner. It can change the dynamics of their interactions and make everyone feel uncomfortable. You can never be sure if your problems aren't being broadcast across town. Relationship problems are never made better through gossip and conjecture. It can deeply hurt the one you love to hear rumors. If you need to confide in a friend, try and follow these rules:

- Make sure it's a friend you really trust.

- Keep it as a generalized question, if possible.

- Never heap all of the blame on your partner.

- Make it understood you are looking for a solution, not to end the relationship.

Reserve Time for Friends and Your Partner

Balancing your free time is the crucial component to making friends and your partner happy. Check ahead with your mate to make sure it's okay to go ahead and make plans to go see a movie or head out to a basketball game. Encourage your partner to try and find time to spend with their friends occasionally. Having interests outside the relationship help keep the growth continuing. Here are a few ways to make this impossible trick possible:

• Make sure your partner has met and is comfortable with the friend you will be hanging out with occasionally. Invite them over for dinner a few times.

• Plan events as far in advance as possible.

• Make these outings a reasonable amount and length of time.

• Never cancel plans with your partner to spend time with your friends.

• Give priority days and times to your partner. Maintain the traditions and rituals you've started to create.

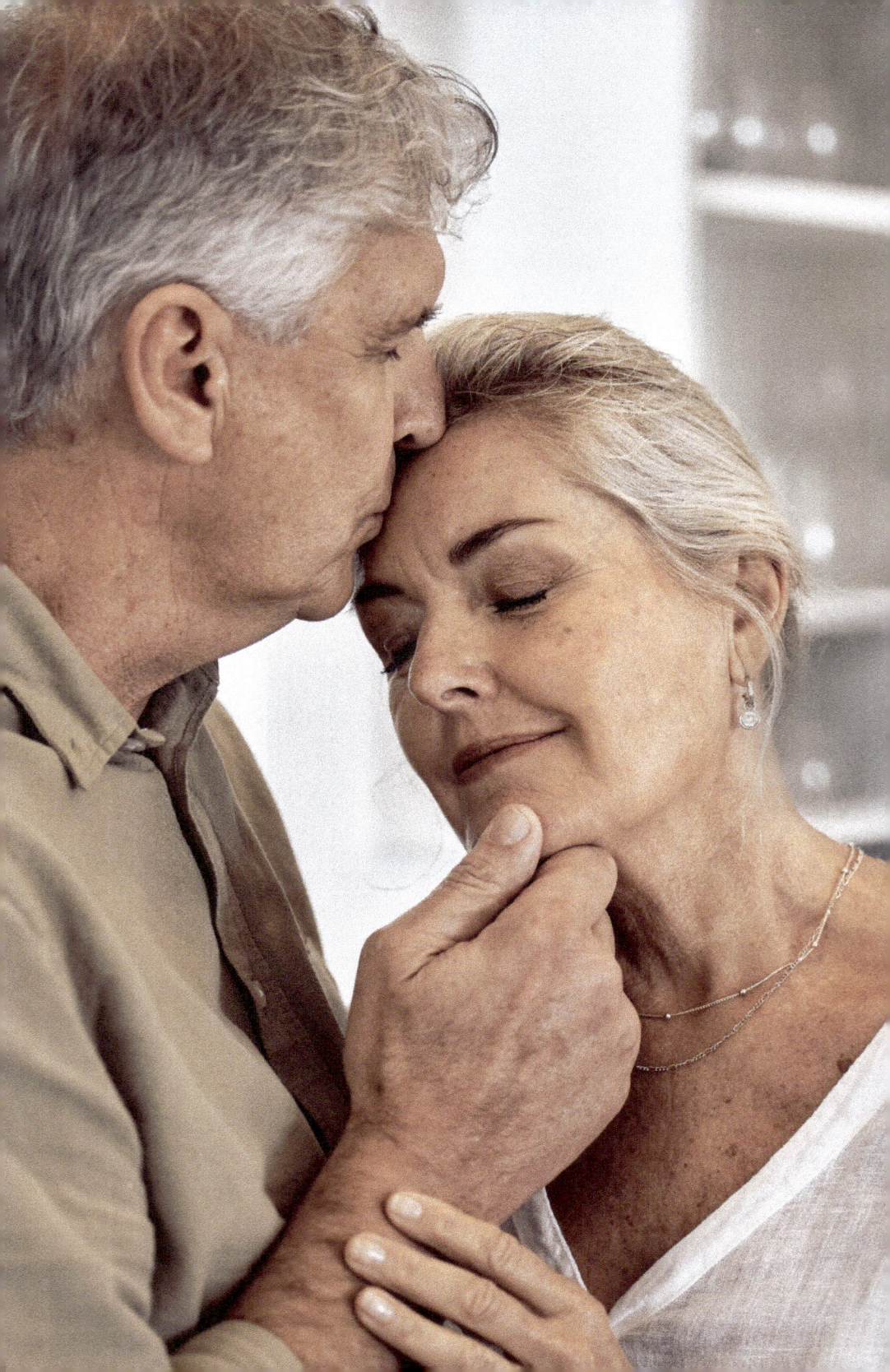

Chapter 12: Become an Expert About Your Partner

The more you know and are willing to learn about your partner, the closer you will become and at a much faster pace. Finding a few bits of information to identify with will help offer you reassurance that you've found your forever mate. You don't want to be identical twins about everything, but a few things in common gives you an instant bond. Some areas such as goals and values are important to be on the same page for relationship success.

Know the History of Your Partner

Knowing a few of the basics in the history of your partner and openly sharing your history will give each of you a foundation to begin exploring more in-depth. You can't be expected to remember everything in the beginning but build on information as time goes by. A few of the things to start with could be:

- Where they were born.
- Where they grew up.
- The size of their family.
- Where their family is located.
- Education level.
- Profession and job experiences.
- Any past serious relationships/marriages.

- Any children and where they are located.

A small amount of information to start will allow you to initiate conversations that lead you to learn even more. It's important to have enough information to feel comfortable that you are making a great choice in partners.

Discuss Life Ambitions and Goals

What are your goals in life? Are you wanting to live in a big city or have dreams of a small cottage near the woods? Do you like fancy cars, or is an old 4X4 pickup all you'll ever want and need? What are your ambitions with career, home ownership, salary, retirement plans, and savings? You can find out the same information in return. It's vital to ensure you and your partner have ambitions and goals that line up with one another or you will end up a miserable person.

Know their Core Values and Whether they Line up with Your Own

Core values are the value you place on things like honesty, integrity, work ethic, compassion, and more. It would be difficult to establish a long-term relationship with someone that did a little shoplifting or found lying to be no big deal if those are not your values as well. It's a recipe for immediate disaster. Most core values are established before the age of six, although it doesn't mean that values can't be added to and expanded over the course of your life. It's good to know where you're starting at and see where things align and where there are potential problems.

What are their Tastes in Music, Movies, Books, Food?

Great conversations require a good supply of basic interests and knowing what their tastes are in music, movies, books, food, fashion, and all things current or trendy. The better you share the intricate likes and dislikes of basics in life, the wider the arena is for powerful conversations. It's also nice to know areas you may differ, at least slightly. It can help expose you to something different you might end up loving just as much. Every person that loves Mexican food never realized it until giving it a try. Sharing new experiences forces you to look at your favorites in a new light. It can breathe new life into what had become stagnant.

What is their Favorite Color, Animal, Car, and More?

Keep it going! You aren't finished in the learning process if you are going to become a true expert in your partner. You still need to discover important things like what is their favorite color, favorite car, favorite animal, and whether they prefer gold or silver. It's almost as if a floodgate opens and the conversations become powerful and filled with vital information. It also provides plenty of clues on what you can get for birthdays, holidays, and anniversaries. The sky is the limit in asking the question but try and spread out the questioning over a long period of time.

Are they a Deep Thinker or Impulsive by Nature?

How a person communicates can have a lot to do with their baseline personality. You'll be able to make observations as easily as they can see where you sit on the spectrum. More reserved, deep-thinking individuals often seem to have fewer words to say. They tend to place a lot of emphasis on the words used, however. It could be that they are introverted. It doesn't mean they are shy but more deliberate and selective in action.

A more impulsive person is generally considered an extrovert. Although it may appear to be all over the map, the tasks and conversations are skillful and done in their own special way. You'll find that the more impulsive personalities hardly ever run out of conversational topics. Most are upbeat and highly energetic. Making these simple observations can point you in the best directions for starting and continuing a conversation.

What are Some of their Basic Habits?

Learning a few of their basic habits will help make you an expert on your partner. Do they go jogging every Monday and Wednesday morning? Is there a show they have to watch on Friday evenings? Do they prefer to drink coffee out on the patio on their day off? Do they have an irritating twitch to their eye if you leave a dirty dish in the sin after a midnight snack? Studying and understanding the habits of your partner will help you work more in unison and help create a happy home environment.

What do they Need from a Relationship?

All parts of information you gather culminate in showing you what they are looking for and need from a relationship. Ask the important questions, assimilate the information, and use it to help create a smoother transition into the relationship. (See figure 5)

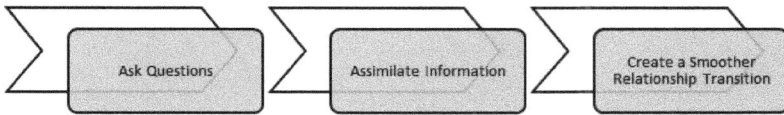

Figure 5 – The process of discovery and learning about your partner.

Learning about your partner should be something you look forward to on a daily basis. Most successful relationships are not based on a perfect fit. It's finding ways to fit together in the uneven areas that make the difference. Finding ways to grow together is the ultimate goal.

Chapter 13: Know What's in Their Suitcase

Every person carries a suitcase of beliefs and ideals that shape the everyday view and perception of the world. Most are not comfortable with showing this to people they are not familiar and comfortable with, including you, initially. Begin unpacking this suitcase and taking a look at the contents at your first opportunity. You must be willing to allow them access to your personal suitcase. Being open and honest in communication is critical to growing together instead of apart.

The Importance of Seeing the Complete Package

The process of unpacking this suitcase and giving each area an inspection begins during the dating phase. It's good to explore what your partner's beliefs are in every aspect of life, love, and human interaction. How well will they get along with people, even beyond their relationship with you? Are they able to hold a steady job and relate well to friends? Are they frequently bumping heads with authority figures? Do they seem mature when it's required? It's important to look at these details to fully understand the big picture. The way they communicate or fail to communicate with others can be a warning sign that things can break down.

Are You Seeing Stable Moods and a Compatible Personality?

Sudden and drastic mood swings in a partner can make life miserable. Do they seem to have a stable countenance most of the time? Women can get thrown off by monthly hormonal changes, but it can also indicate their ability to handle stress and anxiety. Talking about possible stressors and ways to reduce anxiety can help you and your partner. As long as your basic personalities seem compatible, the rest is workable. Your partner will be in awe that you are willing to help them talk through their worries and anxieties.

What Makes Your Partner Emotional?

All people have a different threshold of emotional response to everything in life. Emotional control and the ability to show emotion are equally important in being able to convey feelings properly. Do they have problems discussing emotional subjects? Do you have to be the one to initiate affection? It's important to find a happy medium that allows both of you to feel comfortable sharing and demonstrating emotional response. It may be that your partner needs to venture out of their comfort zone and experience a new way of responding to things.

What are their Pet Peeves?

Pet peeves are little things that drive people absolutely bonkers! It's handy to know what these things are with your partner. You should also relay any of your pet peeves to them. It could something as slight as not loading the dishwasher the way they normally do the job. Learning what the pet peeves are for each of you and avoiding them will help bring a more harmonious atmosphere to the home. Instead of viewing them as a bit of trivial information, think about how you feel when your pet peeve is right in front of you. Shoes left in the middle of the floor, laundry piled in a corner instead of the hamper, or whatever really makes your blood boil.

What are their World Views?

How does your partner view the world? Are there any strong political views that might clash with your own? Are fears of a tanking world economy one of the first things they talk about every morning? The last thing anyone wants first thing in the morning is to hear political ranting and raving. It's worth exploring what their world views are and how you can help minimize any conflict by avoiding particular topics of discussion. It's not the end of the world to hold differing views.

Why Do they Hold their Particular Views?

If your partner holds strong world views and seems majorly opinionated, try and find out why they feel the way they do. It's often a generational idea passed down through families. Are they okay with your views being a little different or less strong? The last thing you want is to feel you have to convert to any beliefs and views you are not comfortable with, any more than they would want to convert to yours. Most people tend to fall somewhere in the moderate range of political and world views. It's rarely a big problem in most relationships.

Is there Any Extra Baggage?

People have a tendency to carry extra baggage with them you can't always detect immediately. It could be old hurts carried over from a disastrous relationship or marriage. It might be from suffering abuse as a child. Incidences like this that leave pain and trauma can affect how they respond and deal with people. It can lead to problems with trust or fears of abandonment. You need to listen for a few key words when all of these various topics are discussed. Some words to look for are:

- Divorce – parental or their own.
- Child custody problems.
- Child abuse.
- Spousal or partner abuse.
- Alcoholic or drug addict upbringing.
- Cheating partner.

How to Become an Expert Baggage Handler

The fact that someone is carrying a little extra baggage doesn't make them a bad potential partner. It might take time and patience to completely win over their trust. Your partner might automatically begin to feel high levels of anxiety if you don't make it home right when expected and rush to think you're cheating. Keep your cell phone handy and call if you are running late. A little gesture like this will help put their mind at ease and keep them out of older, bad place.

Chapter 14: Coping with Problems Together

No matter how right you live your life, problems will come and go. Some are much bigger and meaner than others. It's essential that you determine to help one another cope with and work through problems together. Anything less is not a true commitment to the relationship. Your biggest tool in coping and solving problems is by maintaining good communication. It's impossible to read your partner's mind. You need the benefit of dialogue.

Don't Hide Problems from One Another

Never hide problems from your partner. If it's bad enough they'll find out anyway over time, unless you plan on disappearing. Most problems can be reigned in pretty quickly if you can work as a team from the start. Hiding a problem will only allow it to grow. It might be tempting to try and hide the problem if you're afraid it will bring you shame, such as over-drafting your bank account. It won't make it go away any faster. A few benefits of telling your partner about problems as they arise are:

- You no longer have to worry about it alone.

- Your partner might be able to come up with a quick solution.

- You get immediate support, which you might need.

- You cultivate trust with your partner.

- Two heads can figure out a solution quicker than one.

Don't Shut Down Mentally or Emotionally

The extreme stress and anxiety that follows the realization that a big problem is looming can threaten to shut you down emotionally or mentally. You have to fight to stay in the game and give useful assistance to your partner in resolving the issue. You may find yourself not wanting to talk, sulking, or sleeping more. You need to shake off the feelings of depression and gloom to move forward. You don't have the option or luxury of giving up on a situation if it affects your partner as well.

A serious problem like finding out your home is going into foreclosure can be traumatizing. You may have instinctually known the time was coming, but it's different to see everything in black and white print. It's understandable but you have to get moving quickly to manage things. Whether it's resolving the foreclosure or finding another place to live, time is of the essence.

Outside Problems Need a Unified Front

The great thing about being in a relationship is that you can truly work as a unified front against any outside problems that try to move in on your turf. Neither one of you has to deal with situations alone. Even though it might seem like a difficult battle, it allows you the privilege of getting closer and feeling more like a team. It can be one of the best things to happen when it comes to strengthening your relationship. It also carries the possibility of tearing the relationship apart if you don't work together. Instead of taking on the true enemy, you'll tear each other down or place blame. Neither is productive or gets you to the solution.

Relationship Problems Require Communication

Problems that develop within the relationship will need good communication to resolve. It may not be the immediate solution, but it begins to peel away the layers of problems that get a relationship in a tough spot. You have to openly and honestly tell each other how you feel and what you think the solution looks like. The longer you put off talking, the more bad feelings and hurt will fester. Even if you don't feel like talking right away, come to the peace table as soon as it seems sensible to do so. Quiet and disconnect only causes more pain.

Try and Talk Without Anger

No matter how aggravated and irritated you feel, set the anger aside long enough to talk things through calmly. Anger only clouds judgment and gets in the way of real progress. Anger is usually a mask for hurt and should be stifled for the duration of talks. A few things to keep in mind when talking to help minimize anger:

- Look for a solution rather than focusing on blame.

- Keep your voice lowered and calm.

- Keep all emotions out to minimize the likelihood of an anger outburst.

- Make the needed apologies.

- Try to see things from the other perspective.

- Look for resolution rather than getting even.

- Break off talking temporarily if anger cannot be curbed. Take a walk outside or get a drink of water.

Focus on all the positive reasons you are in a relationship to keep negative feelings from making a showing. Don't give up!

Don't Walk Away with Unresolved Problems

Don't make the mistake of walking away from the relationship when there are still unresolved problems. It's a move that you will regret at a later time when you have a chance to think about it more rationally. Without the right amount and types of communication, any problem can seem insurmountable. It's even more intimidating if there has been a lack of good communication for a period of time. Take a fresh breath of air and stay calm about the situation. Making rash decisions might give you the resolution you feel you need at the moment, but it can cost you a valuable relationship by giving up.

Find Solutions Like Compromising

Spend a good amount of time seeking out and discussing possible solutions to the problems. Not every situation can be handled the same way, but there is one thing all solutions have in common. It took good hard work and dialogue to reach the end. If nothing else, see if you can somehow come to a compromise. The best way to do this is:

• Write out a list of the problem or problems and be very detailed.

• What are the consequences of not finding a solution?

• What are the benefits of reaching a solution?

• What are some ways that each side can compromise a little to reach common ground?

• What are the possible obstacles to compromise?

• How committed are you to reaching a firm solution?

Do your best to work through the problems slow and honestly. Involve an impartial third party if you feel it might help.

Chapter 15: Appreciate, Accept, and Valorize Your Partner

It's easy to get caught up in the fast-track of life and forget to do the simple things like letting your partner know how much they add to your life. Little moments of showing basic appreciation are what make the tougher moments easier to swallow. No one wants to keep forging forward under heavy fire if they feel their partner doesn't really care or even notice they are around. It's time to begin making plans to start showing more appreciation each and every day.

Appreciation Can Mean Everything

Little gestures made at the end of the day that show your partner you are thinking of them and appreciate what they do can mean the world after a long day at work, struggling with putting kids to bed, and trying to fit in some snuggle time before bed. Saying a simple and honest "thank you" with a smile can make a real difference in your relationship. It helps refuel you to tackle another day. It takes almost no time out of your day to give their hand a squeeze, look them in the eye with a smile and tell them you appreciate them. A quick hug or a peck on the cheek can also put a big smile on their face, male or female.

Be in Awe of All Your Partner Does for You

Besides your mother, who else would run out in the dead of winter to get you some cold medicine? Who else would put a blanket over you when you are so exhausted you fall asleep on the couch? Who else would come out to where your car broke down, try and fix it, call a tow service and still get you to work on time? The litany of things our beloved partner does as a matter, of course, each day should leave you in awe of this near superpowers.

Too often the things you do go unnoticed or unrecognized. Have you ever felt your presence is only recognized when you've done something wrong? You need to move away from this habit as a couple. It sets a dangerous precedent of taking one another for granted. Once this starts, it's a long way back to the station. Start taking notice of the little things that are done that you never thought about. Clean laundry is always available in the dresser. The house is always reasonably clean. The yard is always mowed, and the plants watered. The vehicles always have oil changes and antifreeze added when necessary. All of the things you haven't done yourself have been done by your partner. Feel awe in that.

Accept Your Partner – Beauty and Flaws

You've heard it said a million ways that no one is perfect. Not in looks or deeds. Sometimes you roll out of bed cranky and don't want to be bothered. Other times the world looks like it's made of solid gold. As much as beauty is in the eye of the beholder, so is acceptance. Everyone needs to feel accepted by their mate for their bad hair days and when they are dressed to go out on the town. Makeup and fancy suits shouldn't be the entrance attire to sit down for a home-cooked meal and pleasant conversation. Home should be the one place that everyone can relax and let their hair down.

Taking life too seriously can cause you to miss out on the best opportunities you have to show your partner they are loved – unconditionally. The flaws and imperfections should be what endears them to you more than any perfections. It should be the complete package that you find attractive. Anything less and you need to begin questioning your own motives for being in a relationship. Keep all the reasons close that you fell in love with your partner. It can carry you through some tough times.

Give Your Partner Just Dues for their Value in Your Life

How much do you value the partner you have? Can you imagine making it down some of the rough roads you have with anybody else? Single people are everywhere, but you were drawn to your partner for special reasons. They aren't like everybody else. Make it a point to always give credit where credit is due. If your partner figures out the solution to a tough situation, give them full rights to the deed. Brag about how amazing your partner is to your family, friends, co-workers, or the postman. Your partner might tell you to stop but deep down it makes them incredibly happy that their actions are recognized.

You don't have to go overboard to the point of sounding sappy, but really pour it on when it's warranted. It can leave your partner floating on cloud nine for days. It makes it that much easier for them to go the extra mile again. It's another part of developing a lifelong friendship that is nearly impossible to break apart. It's one of the secrets to marriages that last 50 and 60-years. No one ever feels slighted or taken for granted.

Every detail has been observed, mentally accounted for, and appreciated.

Show How Much You Care Daily

You should never wait until after arguments and in the process of making up to show your partner, they are dearly loved. Find a special way to show them how much you care every day. The next day is never promised, so this might be the last chance you have. Make it count. A few ways to show you care are:

- Make your partner a special breakfast.
- Take their car to the gas station the night before and fill up the tank to save them time the next morning.
- Leave a special note on the bathroom mirror.
- Dads- let mom sleep in and get the kids up for school.
- Take your partner out for brunch or lunch.
- Turn a music channel on the television and dance with your partner.

Never let a day go by without finding a way to show how much you value their friendship, companionship, hard work, and love.

Chapter 16: Practice Empathy

U nless you live under a rock, at some point you are going to have to deal with emotionally charged situations. It might make you feel awkward and uncomfortable, but your partner will need your full support in these moments. You may need the support of your partner during an emotional time. The first part of mastering empathy is to find out what it is and why it's so important.

What is Emotional Empathy?

Emotional or primitive empathy is our natural desire to respond to the heightened emotional state of another person. It's the urge to cry when someone gets bad news and begin to have a strong emotional reaction. Women seem to be more naturally attuned than men, but men can easily develop an empathic ability with the right understanding. It may not feel completely comfortable at first, but it's crucial to have empathy for your partner and vice-versa. Without empathy, your partner might feel like you have no feelings for them or their situation at all.

What is Cognitive Empathy?

Cognitive empathy is our conscious ability to sort through the emotions we are witnessing and attempt to make the right decision on reactions. Our brains can begin deciphering a situation faster than you might believe. You may not know what happened but hearing someone wailing and crying in a public area is an alert that something terrible has happened and the person is unable to control their emotions in that instant. Your emotional empathy kicks in and you at least mentally gravitate towards that person out of compassion. You may never approach the person, but your entire nervous system is on edge and wants to respond.

What Triggers Empathy?

Any strong burst of emotion can trigger empathy to the one witnessing the scene. Anger, laughter, sadness, physical weeping, visible tears, and sobs can all help trigger the emotional empathy response in humans. Anger and sadness are the two strongest emotions that trigger typical responses. Once it's triggered, you are left with the options of ignoring it or getting into action. Learning how to correctly use your empathy response can be a useful skill in a relationship. A few things that can bring about the need for empathy response are:

- A painful injury.
- Death of a loved one.
- Death of a pet.
- Loss of a job.
- Arguments
- Any devastating or shocking event.

Any of these can happen at any time to your partner and you should prepare to handle them with ease and comfort. It can be the one thing that brings you in a closer bond to your partner than ever before.

How to Understand Your Partner's Emotional State

The easiest way to understand your partner's emotional state is to ask what happened and compare it to feelings you would naturally have if it had happened to you. It's literally a moment where you need to mentally walk in their shoes briefly. Tears and crying will clue you in on it being something sad or traumatizing in nature. Loud voices, yelling, or screaming could indicate it's an argument of some sort. Most people will offer a clear visual presentation that is hard to mistake for the emotional state they are in, especially with the stronger emotions.

How to Better Respond with Empathy

When your partner is visibly angry, your best option is to try and talk them into a calmer state. Arguments with family members, friends, neighbors, or complete strangers can happen at the drop of a hat. When tempers flare it's hard to get everything calm. You can say things like "I understand why you feel this way, but you should calm down." Enough prodding with a look of concern should do the trick within a few minutes time unless the person they were arguing with is still present. Try and whisk them away from sight.

An unexpected bad event that has your partner in tears can be difficult to watch. Most adults don't cry unless it's a completely devastating event like a death or serious loss of some type.

Hugs and reassuring them that everything is going to be okay is one way to be there and show empathy.

How Compassion and Empathy Makes You a Better Life Partner

Life is known to throw a curve ball or two and painful or aggravating things will happen. As much as you'd love to shield your partner from all of the bad in life, it's a futile exercise. Family members and pets grow old and pass away. Serious illnesses and accidents happen every day. Road rage and angry neighbors are an almost daily vision on the nightly news. You can do the next best thing and be prepared to offer an empathic support system for these types of scenarios. Your partner will always remember and cherish your help through difficult moments.

Dealing with Heavy Emotional Moments

No one likes the thought of having to deal with heavy emotional situations, especially when it involves your partner. It's times like this that take compassion, understanding, and wrapping them in love and light to begin feeling better. Don't spend a ton of time talking. Allow your partner to talk when they are ready. If they are angry over an argument, let them gradually cool off and fume. Allow them the luxury of having someone to talk to that they trust and know understands the situation. Grief will pass with time, but your partner will remember you were there when they needed the support the most.

How to Communicate You Understand with Sincerity

Having established bonds with your partner will help demonstrate sincerity on your part. It might be difficult for someone that doesn't know you, but your partner should have no doubts. Allowing your partner an opportunity to cry or vent as they need to and seek your comfort, consolation, and input at their own pace helps. No amount of saying "I'm sorry" will bring back a loved one and it's sometimes better to stay somewhat silent. Your reassuring touch and hugs will do more to help them feel supported than anything you can say in the moment.

Chapter 17: Cope with Defenses

One unpleasant truth about most people is that they don't really like to hear criticism, even if it's well-deserved. It can make the hackles go up and put you on the defense. Finding ways to communicate that get around this somewhat natural tendency is a good idea if you want smooth sailing in your relationship. It matters in how you deliver criticism and the level at which you feel like harping on a subject. No one wants to be lectured over and over about anything.

Why Do People Get Defensive?

Hearing that you've done something wrong, said something wrong, put something in the wrong place, or didn't do a good enough job can hit at the personal pride level. You may feel that everything is fine and to hear strong criticism can get your defenses in high-gear, even if it's your partner saying the words. It's times like these that you need to stop and take a deep breath. Taking a little criticism personally is not going to be beneficial in any way to your day or help you get everything done before bedtime.

The brain seems to want to naturally head into protective mode if one thing is said negatively about anything you've done or said. Sure, it's non-productive, but happens almost in the blink of an eye. It can be hard to stop a defensive statement from crossing your lips. In these moments you need to ask yourself one question. "Is it a fair assessment?" A closer inspection of something or thinking back on your words might prove interesting. It could be that the criticism is deserved. It doesn't excuse your partner from delivering it rudely if that's the case, but it can help you lower your defenses back down to a tolerable level.

What Triggers the Need to Feel Defensive?

Everyone loves to think they do a great job at all things, at least a majority of the time. It's hardly the truth, but it's what your mind spews back at you if someone dares criticize your work, actions, or speech. Some people are more sensitive to criticism than others. Feeling rushed, overwhelmed, or tired can also contribute to feeling triggered to get defensive. It's not so easy to maintain emotional control when several of these factors are at play. Being in an off mood can also contribute to the argument that might ensue after your partner berates you for any reason.

Extroverted partners are more likely to give you a spicy response to criticism. Anyone that is busy trying to get a lot of stuff done in a short amount of time might also feel triggered. The response level of everyone is different and widely varies by circumstance and temperament. One guarantee is that the triggering partner will have their hands full if it's the right day and the wrong thing to say. It rarely leads to serious arguments but can cause hurt feelings and feelings of resentment, even if only temporary.

How to Minimize Defense Posturing in Yourself and Your Partner

One of the best ways to defeat a rush to a defensive posture in yourself is to approach criticism with a little humor. If your partner hands you a plate you washed, and it still has a crumb of food on it, set it in the sink and say "Gee, I was saving that for a snack later." It's also a good idea to stop and think about the criticism and how it relates to the scope of everything in the universe. The sun will probably still come up the next morning, even if you didn't get all the wrinkles out of a shirt you ironed.

A sure way to keep your partner from feeling defensive when you offer up a little criticism is, to begin with a compliment. It sets the tone better by bringing positive to the forefront. One example would be the need to point out that a portion of the patio door has streaks after your partner cleans the glass surface. Here is how you can address the situation in a positive way:

"Wow! I haven't been able to see this great out the door in a long time. You did such a great job! Oh, there's a streak over here. It's still a lot better than the last time I did it!"

The positive take on the entire situation tends to diffuse any anger or feelings of hurt. The brain is more reactive to praise.

Criticism and Vulnerability

One thing to remember in your relationship is that you and your partner will be open with one another, which leaves you somewhat vulnerable. It can be a large contributing factor to feeling hurt by criticism. You feel that your mate would always be in your corner, no matter how terrible the vacuuming job. When reality hits that they see you for all your positives AND your faults, it can sting. Is the criticism surrounding anything that's a pet peeve to them? Water stains on glasses are all it takes sometimes. Pick your battles wisely and choose to move on.

The effort it takes to choose not to live in a state of offense is often greater when you are lacking sleep and are just pushing your day too hard. Stop and consider this possibility before getting into arguments about criticism and critical feedback. It may not seem like a big deal when looked at under the scrutiny of a well-rested mind.

Chapter 18: Anger Management

Managing anger is one of the more essential tasks to complete if you or your partner has a problem with controlling this emotion. Unchecked anger can do more damage to your relationships in a short amount of time than almost anything. It can lead to acts of violence, mistrust, and possible arrests. Even though anger is a natural emotion, lack of control with anger is where many people end up on the deep side of the proverbial pool.

Being Quick to Anger

Let's face it, some people are quick to anger no matter what the circumstance. Are you or your partner one of these people? Unchecked anger can lead to making decisions that are impulsive and not constructive when it comes to arguments. It's a large reason you see tires slashed, windows broken, and homes set on fire. Thankfully, most cases don't rise to this extreme level of anger, it can still do untold damage to your relationship. You can push away a good partner who becomes sick of dealing with the roller coaster emotional ride of an angry person.

The best thing an angry partner can hope for is having an established relationship with someone that's slow to anger. It helps provide the balance needed to give the relationship a fighting chance to survive. Even the calmest person can only take so much of an out-of-control anger tirade on a nightly basis. The cycle of anger, angry action, and calm, only to have it cycle again, over and over, will burn out the most patient of partners. (See figure 6)

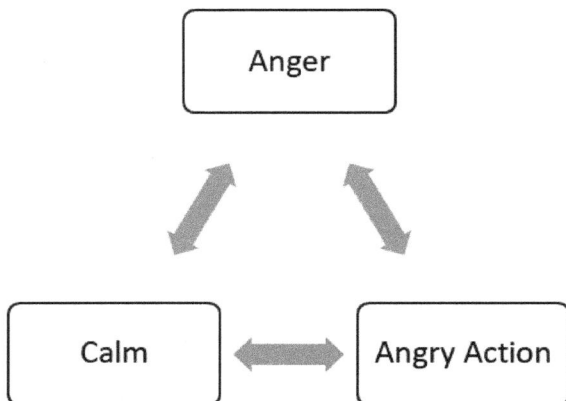

Figure 6 – Cycle of anger, angry actions, and resulting calm.

Set Rules to Not Hurt Partner or Throw Things

It's never acceptable to Allow anger to convince you that picking up and throwing items or hurting your partner is okay. You need to establish baseline rules to make hurting your partner unacceptable. You should never have to fear for your safety because your partner is unwilling to set boundaries. Anger is like any other emotion. It will take over if you are unwilling to reign it in. You can sit and try and relax or allow it to grow and become worse. Failure to recognize your ability to control emotions is what makes it easy for the problem to revisit.

Separate into Different Areas if Things Get Heated

Listen for the bell and go to your separate corner like fighters do in the ring, especially if you don't feel the anger is going away. Most bouts of what's considered' irrational anger" fade after the first few minutes of an angry encounter. Anything longer than this requires the individual to keep it stoked in the mind. Move off to another area of the home or take a walk if you or your partner is not able to bring anger levels down. Leave your partner alone if you know they are struggling with anger issues and have moved off to cool down.

Never Hurl Insults, Curse or Call Names

Developing a bad habit of cursing at your partner or hurling nasty insults is nothing to be proud of. It is a short walk down the common-sense lane to realizing at some point your partner will leave permanently or a trip to jail will happen. The calmest of partners might feel a little sorry for your lack of self-control, but they won't continually put up with the disrespectful nature of verbal abuse. You have to cultivate enough self-control that a line is drawn in the sand that allows you plenty of leverage to gripe about things without stepping off the edge of an anger cliff.

How to Deal with an Angry Partner

The first thing to recognize in an angry mate is that you are not responsible for their inability to keep anger in check. You may be hearing from them that everything is your fault, but is it really? It's possible that something you did or said stirred them to anger, but you can't take it on the chin to feel the guilt of their inability to keep anger at a reasonable level. Here are a few tips to consider when dealing with an angry partner:

• Remove yourself from the situation if anger has gotten out of control and they won't leave.

• Discontinue discussions if any items have been hurled or you are being yelled at.

• Revisit the discussion after a good night's sleep.

• Let your partner know you love them but will not tolerate unacceptable levels of anger.

• Pray for your partner to be released of the feelings of anger.

How to Avoid Being an Angry Partner

Studies by every known psychology center have all concluded the same results when it comes to unchecked levels of anger and relationships. The partner subject to the anger is always deeply impacted. It can be traumatizing without ever having a finger placed on them in the anger. The mental and emotional damage are enough. Seek professional help for your anger if you don't feel you're managing it well enough on your own. Follow a few basic tips to keep yourself and your partner safe:

• Know when the anger is no longer productive, but

hurtful.

- Don't use anger as a way of seeking revenge.

- Keep your hands in your pockets if you are afraid you will lose control.

- Determine to never cross the line into harming a partner.

- If you are unable to think clearly with anger, it's not the right time to talk.

Chapter 19: Learn to Apologize in a Conscious Way

Feeling hurt by your partner for any number of reasons can be healed quickly by a deep, heart-felt apology. Why does it seem too difficult for some to take this small step that would mean the world to their partner? Many seem to assume that you understand they are sorry by continuing to stay in the relationship. Unfortunately, this s not the case. Instead of being called to the carpet, the partner will continue along as if the incident never happened. It will eventually erode away the faith a person places in the relationship.

The Power of Being Apologetic

True power does exist for those that take the steps of apologizing for misdeeds, or any number of infractions on their partner. Taking ownership of your bad behavior or decision-making is the only way to experience real freedom from the more sinister side of life. Getting caught up in the heat of the moment of an argument can lead to harsh words being said that were never meant. Once the words are spoken, they cannot be unspoken. Leaving that kind of hurt out there unaddressed is not only wrong – it's just not cool. It stands firm in the mind of your partner.

You need to take the step of rectifying the situation through an apology. Even the most laid back of partners will begin to doubt your sincerity when you can't even seem to muster the energy to say you're sorry. Your words will hold less and less value over time. It has a direct chilling effect on any relationship, no matter how young or old the participants. The inability to own up to the problem is another symptom that is keeping your partner trapped in a vacuum that doesn't recognize the cost of the damage they do. Not being willing to take a look at your own faults ensures you will walk the same path again.

When You Never Hear the Words "I'm Sorry"

All couples have their moments of disagreement and arguing. It's the nature of being two different people that are not always going to agree. Stepping out of bounds in deeds and words is not unusual in this type of scenario, but what happens when the battle is over? Never are there any real winners, but you would think at least some form of apology would be forthcoming. At times, this is exactly what happens. An apology is made, and everything moves along as normal.

The lack of formal apology doesn't give you the closure needed to know you are back on the same page. It's needed to assure your partner you are still on the same team. It may not be responsible for bringing marriages to an end, but it can quickly begin to erode the trust between partners. It leaves the one you love having to guess whether you were sorry for what you did and said or not. Many will assume their partner is sorry, but wouldn't it be better to remove any doubts from their mind? Five-seconds can save the damage of ignoring costs.

Healing Hurt Through Apology

One step in the 12-step recovery program for alcoholism is to apologize to everyone in your life that was hurt by your behaviors when under the influence. Why is this a critical step in the process of recovery? Because it works. It can bring old support systems back to life that were long ago disconnected. The remarkable healing power of hearing someone tell you they are genuinely sorry for hurting you is undeniable. Hurting someone you love, even unintentionally, can have very long-term consequences. Although the words "I'm sorry" hold no physical power, the ability to completely transform a situation gives them added importance.

Truly Being Sorry

A certain percentage of people that never apologize to their partners feel they have nothing to apologize for. A school of thought does exist that pretty much states that no matter how hurtful and damaging the other person feels your words are, the person is far better off having said what they said. It's a completely unapologetic way to manage their lives that can destroy relationships in one fell swoop. Others are not even aware they have hurt you in any tangible way, so no apology has ever been mounted. Awareness and perception are not always equal in relationships.

Bridging the Pain and Regaining Trust

Most apologies with couples come after one or the other has done something or said things that are hurtful. It typically is a repeat offense that draws the ire needed to secure an apology. The apology is an important part of the process in healing the pain caused by the offending action or words. It lets the partner know they can be safe, and that rebuilding trust is possible. It provides a way to start fresh with a clean slate. It's the perfect solution for those dealing with anger issues. So many bad things can be said during bouts of uncontrolled anger that have the power to penetrate the heart and cause deep wounds.

Systematic purging of the mind and soul of hurtful words and actions, mixed with a liberal share of honest apology, can be the exact healing ingredients needed to feel whole again. You should never shy away from apologizing to your partner if you have done or said anything hurtful. It's better to be careful than careless, especially when it comes to the hearts of those you love. No one can be expected to act and think perfectly, but there's no excuse to not make things right when given the chance.

Chapter 20: Learn to Forgive in a Conscious Way

F eeling that you've forgiven someone is not quite the same as knowing you have forgiven. What is the difference? Knowing you have forgiven keeps it at the conscious level. Leaving it at the "feelings" level places it in the background and can lead to real problems in the future. Forgiveness is a necessary process to undergo to keep a relationship healthy and conflicts to a minimum. Learning to consciously forgive your partner can completely enrich your life together. The benefits extend far beyond the immediate moment in time.

What is Forgiveness?

Forgiving someone is a way of letting go of any hurt done against you by an individual and finding a point to clean the slate and move forward. It's important for you to master this when it is time to be a couple. It's not impossible to imagine the offenses and hurts you might commit against one another within the first year, let alone a lifetime. You are two individuals coming together from different worlds and can unintentionally inflict pain. It can be a frequent event until you gain knowledge about what each person views as hurtful and not.

The debate always rages about whether someone should forgive another person. The person you are forgiving might not "deserve" to be forgiven. Forgiveness is not an action done to benefit the person you hurt. It benefits YOU that has experienced the pain. It gives you the ability to recognize you're letting the pain go and gives you permission to move on to a new day. You can't expect others to offer you forgiveness if you maintain a hardline policy of never forgiving anyone else. It doesn't give the other person permission to hurt you more. It simply acts as a sort of reset.

Intentionally Choosing to Forgive

Once you have established the importance of forgiveness to your emotional health and healing, it becomes apparent how crucial it is to regularly forgive your partner. It's your best hope of being forgiven for the moments you falter and do things or say things that are hurtful. You always hope that your partner does nothing to intentionally hurt you, but humans are imperfect. Having a proactive approach and plan in place is the best way you can protect yourself from the pain that unexpected situations entail. Forgiveness is an option that is only dependent on your willingness to participate.

The intentional act of forgiveness is a way to let go of the stress and anxiety that come with relationship problems that aren't necessarily in your control. If your partner cheats on you, it can't be undone. The choices are to stay in a place of anger and resentment or forgive and move forward. Whether the relationship survives or not, forgiveness is necessary for your own peace of mind. Being able to take yourself outside the bitterness, anger, hurt, and feelings of betrayal promotes real healing. It's one of the kinder things you can do for yourself.

It doesn't have to be about anything as dramatic as infidelity. Forgiveness for the smaller things is just as refreshing to the soul.

Leave Previously Forgiven Items Out of New Arguments

If you forgive your partner for something, let it be a done deal. It' not fair to come back months later or even a year down the line and bring all the old rat skeletons out of the closet. If the problem has a recurring theme, it's good to use it for self-awareness. You can only justify bringing up the case at the time. Using old, past events and situations is an unfair fighting technique that proves destructive for most relationships.

Another unfair tactic is to make the partner stay in a place of always feeling guilty. Forgiveness is freedom for both to move on from a bad place in a healthy way. People rarely need reminders of things they've done that weren't great decisions. Most people beat themselves up pretty bad about things. Your constant reminder only shows you didn't truly forgive. Instead, you've allowed bitterness to take root. You need to revisit your feelings on the situation and find out why you are stuck in that place. Until you can reconcile and truly forgive, you'll remain in that bitter spot.

Forgiveness and Moving Forward

Forgiveness is something that allows everyone in a relationship to stay in positive forward motion, regardless of the wrong way things are handles at times. You can tell when your partner is feeling bad about something they said or did. It only makes sense to completely forgive and blot it out. The best way to reduce conflicts in a relationship is to find every way possible to not stay in offense about anything. It impacts your mental, physical, and spiritual health. Forgiveness is the perfect cure for an offense. It fits right in with treating others the way you want to be treated.

The mistakes made in relationships provide excellent opportunities for learning and growth, both as a couple and as individuals. It takes time to learn how to interact with each other in the ways that are preferred, and it might mean doing something wrong now and again. Establishing a basis of forgiveness and allowing your partner to know that one or two mistakes aren't going to ruin the deal is essential to long-term survivability. The bottom line is you can't expect perfection from anyone. You'll have to keep looking if you want a partner that will always do everything right, every time.

Chapter 21: Accepting Criticism

C riticism from your partner is not always a bad thing. In the midst of it all, you might find a new and better way to get something done. Not all criticism is positive, nor is it meant to be. As fallible humans, criticism can be used against you when your partner feels slighted about something. It's important to analyze what the criticism is and see if there's a way for it to be useful and instructive.

Why Criticism Hurts

A few people welcome criticism about the things they do and say as a way of measuring their effectiveness and motivation for change or improvement. Getting criticism from those closest to you might produce a different result than from an employer. It's easy to take it personally and feeling of rejection enter into the scene. It could be a problem in how the information is delivered. It's one thing to give your partner construction criticism but doing so in a derisive and teasing way can lead to relationship problems. Everyone wants to feel valued by their partner and not the subject to perceived ridicule.

You always want to feel that the things you do or say will be well-received by your partner, but everyone comes from a different background. Views, tasks, and communication methods can vary and bring about criticism if your mate simply doesn't agree. It can easily lead to hurt feelings and misunderstandings. Trying to remain flexible is the best way to try and handle these moments. You might find that the criticism is justified, even if the delivery was a bit rough. Patience and understanding are important things when it comes to relationships.

Setting Boundaries on Personal Criticism

Personal criticism can be something that undermines the relationship and establishes a way to exercise control over a partner. It doesn't mean that all personal criticism is bad. You have to be careful in not crossing the line of being controlling or use it as a way to put your partner down when you're angry.

You can set the boundaries you need when it comes to personal criticism or criticism that is not designed to impart helpful information. Communicate your disdain for being told things that are not helpful to you or the household. An example of this that happens frequently is regarding weight. Telling your partner that they are no longer attractive due to weight gain and leaving it at that is personal criticism that's not designed to assist in any way. Why not suggest doing a workout routine together or trying a new healthier menu together. Make sure your criticism has reasons and provides positive aspects or includes helpful suggestions.

Reject Weaponized Criticism

Weaponized criticism is something that happens when the relationship hits rocky ground. Criticism can become a natural extension of what seems like non-stop arguments and it can become extremely hurtful. It becomes an easy way to keep the arguments alive, but it can do more damage than the actual arguing. Weaponized criticism often hits below the belt and becomes degrading in nature. If this is beginning to take place in your home, stop and take a step back. Call a truce and begin trying to re-establish normal conversation again.

Bridging Differences and Compromising

A few changes will need to be instituted if hurtful criticism is a common theme in your relationship. You have to find ways to bridge the differences that are causing critical conflict. It will also involve becoming less rigid and restrictive in your thinking. The partner that is being more controlling will have to agree to relinquish some of the control. Without this happening, the future picture is fairly dim. Simply because your mate does a task their own way, which is much different than you, doesn't automatically make it incorrect. Step down off the soapbox and realize that every task has a hundred ways of getting done.

The compromise could be a necessary tool to use to come to a more harmonious point. It can be difficult to let go and let your partner do some of the things around the house if they do them completely different than your trusty "system." As long as the work gets done to satisfactory levels, does it really matter? You could be engaging in battles that waste time, interject confusion, and cause all sorts of hurt feelings. Some battles are not worth waging. You will have to agree to give up a little bit of control, but the other partner can compromise and switch to a method that doesn't drive you completely crazy.

Learning from Criticism

Good and helpful things can be had from the right deliverance and acceptance of criticism. You can communicate information that makes things easier, earns you more respect at work, or teaches you information you never knew. It's a benefit of being in a relationship that fosters growth and healthy companionship. Leave all the toxic banter to those that don't respect the value of having a partner that cares and is interested in being a seamlessly working team. It's essential that your partner feels you are there for them and aren't just being harsh and overly-critical.

You can improve your deliverance of criticism by:

- Begin with compliments and positive input.
- Try and give critical remarks in a non-personal way.
- Add helpful suggestions to finish with a more appealing delivery.

How to accept criticism without feeling personally attacked:

- Find a way to laugh about the situation.
- Consider if the criticism has a basis in truth.
- Try the offered suggestions or find a solution that makes sense.
- Don't absorb it as a personal hit.
- Use it as a schematic for compromise. It can lead to great things and complete peace in the home.

Chapter 22: Trust Your Partner

E ffective communication is a way to increase trust in your relationship. The more you talk about your insecurities, the better your partner can address the areas that cause you concern. The dating world is filed with horror stories of situations that give you pause in wondering whether finding a truly committed partner is possible. You can have a fulfilling relationship that is completely open and maintains healthy boundaries. It's fine to maintain privacy in some things, but as a couple, it's better to be open and share to alleviate fears. It can be difficult for someone that has dealt with cheating issues in the past.

Age of Technology and Trust Issues

More and more, people have their faces buried in their technological devices and enjoy memberships to all different types of social media platforms. The world seems more connected than ever before. Breaking the boundaries of decency and respecting lines are blurred from behind a computer keyboard or smartphone screen. The right combination of ingredients can make it easier for both partners to navigate technology and have everyone feeling confident that nothing bad is going to happen. (See figure 7)

Figure 7 – Step up into a safe and comfortable way to engage in social media as a couple.

Openly Communicate Worries and Concerns

It's impossible for your partner to help reassure you and reduce your worries and concerns about trust if you don't communicate them well. Being open about how you're feeling in all areas of the relationship is a way to continue growing together and customizing behaviors to suit your particular needs. Some people need to have that call every afternoon when the lunch break arrives. Without it, they begin to feel uneasy. Others are perfectly fine to not hear from you all day long. Discuss all of the specific details in regard to staying in contact and finding ways to show one another that you have no intentions of straying from the relationship.

Be Honest

You should always be honest with your partner with any insecurities and worries you have about trust. It's one reason why you should spend a good amount of time learning about your mate and their history. It can give valuable clues for situations that could lead to trust difficulties. Rough former relationships, abandonment issues as a child, child abuse, rape, and more can all indicate that it's best to take great care in making sure they are comfortable with the level of contact they have when you are away.

Share Account Passwords

You should talk about whether sharing passwords for your online accounts would help alleviate the fears of you doing things that could jeopardize the relationship without them being aware. It's not a solution that works for everyone. Some people value their privacy and don't want anyone else to access their emails and bank account. You need to accept their decision and make an honest on for yourself. What would your feelings be on giving your passwords to your partner? Is it going too far? Some feel that you should give blind trust unless they give reasons to start being suspicious.

Text Openly

Sending and receiving texts can be a source of great distress to your partner if they feel you are being secretive about it or dismiss them when asked who you are talking to. Be as open as possible with texting. If you have a client texting to find out information or it's your friend from college, let your partner know to ease their mind. Text your partner from the other room every now and again with something funny or endearing. It will make them smile knowing you're thinking about them, even though they may only be a few feet away.

Keep Flirting Restricted to the Relationship

Save all of your flirty talent and energy for your partner. Keep it in the relationship to get your trust levels up to the top. Too many people feel that flirting outside their relationship is harmless, but it has a chilling effect at home. It can lead to arguments if your mate is somewhat insecure from past hurt. It's not fair or right for you to put them through this type of stress if you already know they are vulnerable. You can use flirting as a way to keep your relationship exciting and strong. A little flirting at home never hurts!

Socialize Together

Go out with friends and have a great time together. Both should spend time transitioning friends to getting to know your partner and understanding that it's a package deal with hangouts. Take your mate with you to company picnics and dinners, holiday parties, and to grab a quick cup of coffee in the morning. Most trust issues tend to fade if they are familiar with and get to know all of your friends. You'll want to get to know all of their friends as well. The mind won't spend time creating scenarios that are not happening if you are called away to help your friends.

Don't Assume Every Partner Cheats

Feeling a bit jaded from former relationships going sour and having been cheated on is normal for a time, but at some point, you have to move on and realize your new relationship is not the old one. Every partner cheating is not an inevitable outcome of relationships. It's a poor choice made by certain people under the right conditions. You have a realistic chance of building a relationship that makes it impossible for the other partner to want to even consider cheating. Constantly assuming they will cheat can push your partner away.

Chapter 23: Revive Your Sex Life

Keeping your sex life happy, healthy, and spiced up makes for a more satisfactory experience. No matter how busy life is, taking time to safeguard and improve your intimate moments are critical to long-term happiness. If you've fallen into a rut as a couple, this chapter might help you find a way to reignite the flame. Our deepest connections on this earth are through the intimacy shared through sexual relations. It's an important part of any lifetime relationship and needs to be given a fair amount of focus.

Eat Healthy and Get Exercise

As far from intimacy as it might seem, getting the right vitamins, minerals, and exercise can make a big difference in how you feel and how well your body performs. Being too tired to have sex is not always a matter of not getting enough sleep. It can happen from a lack of base nutrition and slow metabolism. Get up, get active, and begin making healthy dietary changes and you'll quickly see a difference. Doing healthy dieting or a workout together can be a sexy thing for both partners. Give it a try and see how much it revs up your love life.

Maintain Intimacy Outside the Bedroom

You should spend time each day having some level of intimate contact. It can come in the form of holding hands, hugging, kissing, or sitting next to one another. Direct eye contact, smiles, and silly conversation can help keep that special flame burning bright. Try taking a shower or bath together to keep things interesting outside of the bedroom. If you are the only ones in the house, camp out in the living room or den for a night and see how the immediate change in scenery helps boost your desire for exploration.

Send the Kids Packing

It's hard to feel the freedom to express your sexual desires when there are small kids in the home to look after. Let the kids stay overnight with friends or family, allowing you the free time to have a little fun with your mate. You can feel a little freer with less worry of someone walking in and seeing what they shouldn't. Being free of any obligations can do wonders for a stalled love life. It's often the day to day routines that kill the spin on sexual activity with couples. Imagine how wonderful it might be if you send the kids to summer camp.

Go to an Exotic Location

Enjoying intimacy in areas of the home other than the bedroom is great, but an even deeper way to bask in your affection for one another in a new way is to head off to an exotic location. Waking up to a romantic breakfast in bed in Paris, hearing the waves rolling in at a Mediterranean beachside resort, or watching a sunset from an alpine mountainside villa can be an exciting adventure that picks up your love life. You don't have to go quite as exotic but taking off for a small get-away to a local naturally beautiful setting can be the perfect place to rekindle the romance.

Try New Positions or Toys

Boredom in the bedroom happens when you rely on doing the same things, in the same way, every time. No one feels dietary satisfaction by eating bologna sandwiches day after day. Try soup one day, or a salad the next day. Sex is no different. Do a little research and figure out some comfortable new positions that can help liven things up. Add a few toys to the mix that can help extend playtime. Openly communicate which you like and seem helpful. Being able to concentrate on attempting new things helps ease tensions and has sex more enjoyable.

Send Sexy Messages

Let your partner know every day that you find them sexy and desirable. Send sexy text messages that help put the point home. It can serve two purposes. Not only does your partner know you are in the mood, but it also helps alleviate their fears you might be interested in someone else. Even the most self-confident person can appreciate a message that comes from their partner that stimulates their day. It will make you look forward to seeing one another that night. It has the ability to make you feel like you are on a honeymoon.

Switch to Morning Sex for a Change

Are you and your partner in the habit of having sex at nighttime hours only? It's the most common time to have sex for busy couples. It takes readjustment and finding other opportunities if you find that boredom or feeling too tired in the evening are crimping your sex life. Try setting the alarm to wake you an hour earlier and switch to having sex when first waking up. It might seem foreign the first time or two, but it's a great way to start your day. You can finish by taking a quick shower together.

Set the Mood

The desire to have sex requires being in the mood. You can help set the tone for a relaxing evening that leads to an intimate encounter. Cook your partner a good meal, maybe even open a good bottle of wine. Set the table with candles and turn on some slow, sexy music. Move to the couch and spend time cuddling or spend a little time slow dancing. The evening of complete relaxation and closeness will definitely lead to a satisfying conclusion. You never have to wait for a special occasion to go the extra mile for your mate and make them feel special.

Chapter 24: Set a Few Fundamental Rules

All companies and families operate using an understood set of rules and regulations. Although they don't completely dictate behavior, it does provide the foundation work working relationships within the environment. You must take the time to have a meaningful dialogue about what you want and need for fundamental rules of the relationship. It needs to be an agreeable way to fall back and start from the basics when necessary.

Never Curse at or Berate Your Partner

Cursing and calling your partner foul names only reflects badly on you. It's an unfair way to project all of your anger and anxiety onto the other person. It can take an emotional toll and cause the person to completely withdraw from the relationship. Your partner needs to know they can feel safe in body, mind, and spirit. You should be as protective of their emotions and self-concept as you are of their physical well-being. See the difference a few kind words make.

Never Give Ultimatums or Make Threats

Making an ultimatum or threatening actions to try and get your way is both childish and ineffective. Rather than making demands that are often unrealistic, try conversing and coming to a workable compromise. It gives each side the ability to determine what concessions are livable and allows them to make adult decisions. Treating your partner in a child-like manner will not earn you respect. It will build anger and resentment to points that erupt in arguments. Let the situation get calm and sit down to begin talking things over calmly, with the ultimate goal of peace in mind.

Never Yell and Scream in Front of Kids or Pets

If you are someone that is used to being loud and vocally expressive in arguments, curtail this when pets and children are present. Loud, angry voices scare kids and pets. They may get confused and think they are in trouble or have done something wrong. You are also showing your kids how relationships work. They will grow up feeling that yelling and screaming to get your way is how relationships work. All raised voices and anger add to the situation is more anger and chaos. You can end up with kids and pets that are afraid to approach you when the arguments are over.

Always Attempt to Talk About Conflicts the Same Day it Happens

Try not to put off talking about a sudden problem. Putting things off can make what was a simple problem get more complicated. It makes it easier to put off talking for longer periods of time. The longer the conflict remains unresolved, the more detrimental the results can be. Your partner can hold onto the situation for the next battle and you're suddenly confronted with the new conflict as well as the old one. Spend the time you need to resolve the current conflict quickly. You don't want to have it revisit you later or turn into a bigger deal than it has to be.

Always Talk to Your Spouse About Problems Before Friends or Family

No matter how much you agree to not do it, friends and family will be likely candidates to listen to your relationship woes. Always attempt to discuss the problems with your partner first. If they find out you consulted others without attempting to discuss things at home, you could have just initiated WW3. Your partner will not want problems broadcast to those outside the home because it carries the risk of judgment. You might not paint their behavior in a good light out of anger. It can increase problems between your partner and others in your life.

Never Dive to Personal Attacks

Have you ever been out of words to say in an argument and felt a sudden urge to just blurt out a personal insult to try and gain leverage? It doesn't work and only makes you sound foolish. It gives the appearance that you don't have enough faith in your position to fight with facts. It should never be about winning against your partner. The whole idea behind conflict resolution is to find a workable solution that offers benefits for both and brings peace. Never stray past this proven formula if you really want to see long periods of calm and peace in your home.

Don't Generalize Problems or Behaviors

Making sweeping generalizations about what the person says or how they behave can backfire. Rarely does anyone always talk or act in a specific way enough to label them? Similar issues will call for similar actions, but everyone has to use a myriad of techniques and language skills to solve different issues. Be specific and get to the heart of the matter. Tell your partner the exact words or actions that are troubling to you. Generalizing takes you both farther away from a solution. You'll end up having to dig through and find the actual source of the problem again.

Never Keep Score

If you live life by the scorecard and place a mark for every wrong thing you feel people have done to you, imagine what your card looks like for them. It should be easier for you to recall good things your mate has said or done than the bad. It's hard for a grown partner to take you seriously if you are treating everything like a game. You are not in direct competition and treating your partner like the enemy or opposite team will not yield positive results. Toss the scorecards and discuss things like two adults.

Chapter 25: Write a Couple's Journal

D ocumenting your journey as a couple can be a fun activity that gives you and your family a wealth of information to look back on over the years. You can capture all of those important moments that become fuzzy memories over time. Almost every home, decades ago contained bunches of photo albums. A couple's journal goes beyond by allowing you to document how people feelings about experiences. You can some playful elements that give each partners perspective on the other. It will be a cherished item for any children you have to see their parent's relationship unfold with each page.

Document Milestones

Special occasions like birthdays and anniversaries are to be expected and should be documented. What about times you've graduated from college or training programs? You can add things like the birth of children, moving to a new home, buying a new car, adding a pet to the family, or purchasing a boat. All of the items and occasions mentioned will begin to build a picture of your life. Add pictures, programs, or any other documents that give more information about each milestone. Adding specific details like locations and who is involved will help you recall the occasions and events easily.

Document Vacations

Do you and your partner love to travel for vacations? Make sure and add some space to document these great adventures. It's another area of the journal that will benefit from any images you have, restaurant menus, travel brochures, plane ticket stubs, and more. Where did you go and explain how you made the choice? What did you do while at the vacation destination? List any funny, happy, sad, or aggravating experiences. Document your vacation travel, even if it was only a few miles from home. You can just as much fun and adventure as touring the pyramids in Egypt.

Ask and Answer Daily Questions

Get your partner involved daily in documenting your lives together. Think of and write down a question each day that is both thought-provoking and makes a point. Keep them on the lighter side and pick subjects that will help reveal their personalities. It can be difficult to maintain a daily Q&A but give it a try. You and your partner will begin to look forward to the unexpected question that awaits their attention. Give full answers. Don't get skimpy on the answers just because you had a long or hard day at work. The better you explain things, the clearer it is for those that don't have the benefit of being able to take family vacations.

Likes and Compliments

Add all of the likes of you and partner in the couple's journal to memorialize all of their favorite things. Be sure and speak up on the page with some of your own. You can also create a space within the journal to compliment your partner. Put your thinking cap on and list every little thing you can think of that you like and love about your partner. You can add to this as you go. Have your partner do the same thing about you, featuring every good thing they can think of that endears you in their world.

Daily Recording of Important Events

Every good couple's journal will have areas that are completely dedicated to bringing both specialty subjects or events and the daily grind. Be sure and add little details like the funniest thing to happen that day, any struggles that were overcome, fun activities, and any other major details that make the journal interesting. You will have a lifetime of memories compiled that is incomparable to anything else. Save ticket stubs for movies, concerts and other events you attend and paste them in the journal. You don't have to save everything, but a few to make looking back enjoyable.

Bucket List for Two

Where are all the places you'd love to travel and things you'd love to do as a couple before you die? Create a space in the journal that details all of the wants and desires you both have to see and experience the world. It can be grand plans that never come to fruition, but it gives you real direction in understanding the dreams of your partner. Your partner might dream of climbing Mount Everest together, but you can probably settle for taking a nice hike up a smaller mountain trail on your next vacation.

Sharing Special Goals and Plans

Journaling any special goals and plans you and your partner make is a little different than the bucket list. It should be filled with your goals of home, family, career, vacations, and where you see your life in 5, 10, or 25-years. It can be a comforting area to read if you are experiencing conflict and relationship problems. It can redirect your energies towards working things out. When you can see in black and white how far you've already come, it gives you added energy to go that much farther.

Challenge Your Partner

Being able to present your partner with a challenge can be a fun addition to your couple's journal. Wives can challenge husbands to baking cakes or making a specific type of candy. Husbands can challenge wives to change the oil in the car. It doesn't have to be anything specific. Husbands might already be great at baking cakes and wives at changing vehicle oil. Pick something that each is not accustomed to doing and watch the hilarity begin. It's another spot that would be improved with added images. Get creative but be safe with the activities chosen. You can do these many times over the years.

Conclusion

T hank for making it through to the end of Couple Skills, let's hope it was informative and able to provide you with all of the tools you need to achieve your goals whatever they may be.

Your next move needs to be putting some of these steps into action. Set aside all of your worries and anxiety and get down to the business of saving your relationship. Forget all the drama and negative talk you hear and break everything down into common-sense steps. Marriages and relationships that were considered a lost cause are now thriving after making only a few changes. You will see results right away without spending huge amounts of money on counselors and marriage therapists.

Find a comfortable starting point and begin making changes that will be life-altering. Prepare yourself to be amazed at how easy and enjoyable some of the steps can be. Each day will result in building more trust and understanding from your partner. If both of you are committed to making the changes, the sky is the limit.

Learning to navigate the world as a couple never came with a handbook – until now. You will have the edge in knowing what it takes to make it through any crisis and problem that a couple can face. You'll be able to come out winners every time!

www.ingramcontent.com/pod-product-compliance
Lightning Source LLC
Chambersburg PA
CBHW051246020426

42333CB00025B/3083